The CPA's Guide to a Successful Financial Planning Practice

The CPA's Guide to a Successful Financial Planning Practice:
Selling Financial Investments and Marketing Advisory Services

JIM H. AINSWORTH CPA, CFP, CLU

JOHN WILEY & SONS, INC.
New York   Chichester   Brisbane   Toronto   Singapore

This text is printed on acid-free paper.

This publication is designed to provide accurate and authoritative information in regard to
the subject matter covered. It is sold with the understanding that the publisher is not
engaged in rendering legal, accounting, or other professional services. If legal advice or
other expert assistance is required, the services of a competent professional person should
be sought.

Library of Congress Cataloging in Publication Data:
Ainsworth, Jim H.
    The CPA's guide to a successful financial planning practice,
  selling financial investments and marketing advisory services/Jim
  H. Ainsworth.
        p.   cm.
  Includes index.
  ISBN 0-471-07687-2 (paper)
    1. Financial planners—United States.   2. Financial services
  industry—United States.   I. Title.
  HG179.5.A368   1994
  332.6'068—dc20   94-17917
                                                          CIP

Printed in the United States of America

10 9 8 7 6 5 4 3 2 1

About the Author

Jim H. Ainsworth is president and a cofounder of 1st Global Partners, a diversified financial services firm offering through its subsidiaries, Partners Advisory Services, Inc. and 1st Global Capital Corp., private investment and pension consulting services to individuals and trustees of retirement plans, foundations, and endowments; estate planning; tax counseling; investments and securities brokerage; and insurance and other quality financial services to individuals and businesses.

Jim has been in the financial services industry since 1965. He formed Ainsworth and Lambert, CPAs in 1973. As founding and managing partner, he guided the firm's growth into one of the largest local CPA firms in Northeast Texas. In 1985 he formed Ainsworth Money Management, Inc. and serves as the president and CEO. He became a top producer for his prior broker-dealer for several years and the number one producer for 1990. He served on the firm's advisory board, as a member of The President's Roundtable, and of the Gold Club. Jim also served as vice-president of recruiting and rep development for his prior broker-dealer.

A featured speaker at numerous conventions, workshops, seminars, and other gatherings about financial planning, Jim is recognized nationally for his expertise in adding complete financial services as a profit center for CPA firms. He has produced videos, training manuals, and extensive marketing materials that have been distributed nationwide. He is a certified trainer in sales, marketing, time management, motivational techniques, and personal improvement.

Jim is a Certified Public Accountant, Certified Financial Planner, Chartered Life Underwriter, and Registry Financial Planner. He is a graduate of East Texas State University and is also a NASD General Securities Representative and General Securities Principal and a Registered Investment Advisor. Jim is also a member of numerous professional organizations.

Acknowledgments

My sincere appreciation goes to the staff at Ainsworth Money Management, Inc. for pulling together information accumulated over an eight-year period, and to the staff at 1st Global Partners, Inc. for filling in for me while I worked on this project and for assistance in developing this book.

Thanks also to Jan, my partner in life, and to my children, Damon and Tia, Shelly, Kevin, and Justin, and my grandchildren for supporting me in such a crazy endeavor.

Foreword

I founded a CPA firm in a small town in rural Northeast Texas over twenty years ago. I had held various positions in accounting and related fields for eight years after college. I had no clients and would not have survived had it not been for a small retail store that allowed me borrowing power. I did not have the slighest idea of how to run a CPA firm. I only knew that I had the certificate and that I desperately wanted to be my own boss. Not knowing what was ahead proved to be my salvation. If I had known more about the rigors of starting a small firm from scratch, I might never have started.

Going the extra mile for clients soon started to pay off in referrals. My practice grew enough to add a partner a few years later. Together, we turned the practice into a well-balanced firm with over 600 individual clients and over 100 business clients. We did everything that small CPA firms do—audit, compilation and review, tax, and management consulting. (Actually we mostly talked about management consulting; we never really did too much). In Commerce, Texas, businesses don't hire too many management consultants. We were fortunate to be at the helm of a CPA firm during the Golden Era of the early 80s. We were worried about having more clients and more referrals than we could handle. In the late 80s, we navigated our little ship through a constant barrage of mindless changes in the tax law, overregulation, *more of the same* changes to GAAP and other accounting rules. Finally, we experienced a recession that forced many of our clients out of business. We saw lowballing take away a lot of our audit business, holding companies (and later failures) take away our bank clients, and personal computers take away our write-up and erode our tax business. I don't know that I had any marvelous insight into the future. More out of fear than anything else, I started to market our services feverishly. We tried branch offices in surrounding counties and towns, seminars, mailers, etc. Our faces and names were seen at every event and function for miles around. It worked. We were able to maintain a small growth rate even though our community lost 35 percent of its population during ten years. That small growth rate in revenues was not always accompanied by a small growth rate in the bottom line, however. During this time, the CPA profession was attacking itself with a frenzy of new and burdensome requirements for small CPA firms that added nothing to the quality of our practice—just more expenses that we could not pass on to our clients.

During most of this time, I was trying to do personal financial planning for clients. I produced a few suitably large, academically correct, non-profitable and non-implemented financial plans for clients that I later called "coffee table decorations." I attended the meager offering of financial planning training through my state society of CPAs and the AICPA. These were either taught by folks who wanted the attendees for referral sources or by CPAs who didn't really know how to do financial planning (at least, not for the type of clients that I had). I practiced the *team approach* in those rare instances when I could get a client to implement a financial plan. Meanwhile, my clients continued to have the same problems with their financial lives as before. When tax planning was largely taken away from my clients by changes in the tax law, I felt helpless to enable them achieve their hopes and dreams. The final straw came when I lost a major client due to the actions of one of my *team members*. On that same day, one of my best friends and clients brought in his family tax return already prepared by his sixteen-year-old daughter using tax software that he purchased for half the price I had been charging for his return. That's when I decided I had to change the way I was doing business. I had to learn how to *really do* financial planning and to implement financial plans myself.

That started a wonderful journey that brought me prosperity and returned a sense of accomplishment to my work. Much more important, I started my clients on a journey to financial independence. I hope you will enjoy sharing my experiences in the pages of this book.

Table of Contents

PART **I**

Marketing

TABLE OF CONTENTS

1

Sales and Marketing—TOPS

The acronym TOPS stands for Trust, Opportunity, Pain, and Solution. These are the sequential steps that can make CPAs successful in providing positive services to their clients. In many ways the methods you will learn in the following pages are similar to a number of sales training programs offered today. However, there are also differences. I used and refined these methods for several years without thinking of them as methods at all. Only in the latter years of my unscientific experiment did I find substantiation for the methods I was using in well-researched books.

Most of the articles written today about CPAs entering financial planning say that we will never be a force in this field because we can't sell. They say that we can't develop the kind of relationships required to get a client to do something he doesn't *have to do* because of some law or regulation.

There is considerable support for these arguments. Only a small percentage of the CPAs who belong to the Personal Financial Planning (PFP) division of the American Institute of Certified Public Accountants (AICPA) actually practice personal financial planning. CPAs are showing a definite desire to become more professional and knowledgeable, because large numbers are going after the designations offered through the AICPA and the College for Financial Planning. If so many are getting the credentials, why are so few actually practicing? We can mention the usual excuses of time constraints, liability, and so forth, but they just don't wash. These CPAs knew about them when they started getting the additional education. They clearly have seen the need to add financial planning to their practices in order to foster their own professional growth and because their clients are asking for it.

Much as I hate to agree with the "experts" on this issue, I think that sales reluctance is the primary culprit. That is the limit to my agreement with these pundits, however. They think that we can never overcome our natural tendency away from sales. I disagree.

WHY CPAs DON'T SELL

There are two primary reasons that CPAs don't sell.

1. *We don't like to be sold.* We are uncomfortable in a sales situation when we are the buyer. We detest high-pressure sales in particular. We bristle when we are asked redundant questions such as "If I could show you a way to double your income in 30 days with no effort or expense on your part, would you be interested?" Our left brains start churning and we think, "Of course, anyone would be interested. But if that were possible, you would be doing it yourself instead of selling to me; or whatever you are doing is probably illegal or unethical; or you are lying." We don't like to be asked what color we want or how we want to take delivery *before* we

have decided to buy. Our images of salespeople are tainted by memories of such experiences.

2. *We have previously had to sell our services from a completely different perspective.* The standard response is, "CPAs can sell. They have been selling themselves for years." That's true, but the perspective from which we sold seems different to us from selling financial services and products. Why?

a. Our clients had to have our standard services. There was not a question as to whether they would buy, but *from whom* they would buy. They didn't necessarily have to have financial planning and investment products.

b. The services we sold were largely negative. We found comfort in the "us against them" position as defenders of our clients from the IRS or other regulatory authorities. Investments and financial planning constitute a positive service. The approach comes from another set of emotions. We no longer have a common enemy. In fact, we may perceive the enemy to be ourselves if we don't do everything just right.

c. For the most part, our regular services could be provided only by us or other professionals like us. We knew who our competitors were and how we compared with them. With financial products, there is a new level of competition where we are not totally convinced of our superiority.

d. The complexity of tax law and accounting rules kept our clients at "a comfortable distance." We were secure in knowing that they didn't know what we were doing. With investments, the client gets right in the middle of our business. The involvement is much more personal and pushes us out of our comfort zone.

e. Because of our preconceived stereotypes of salespeople, we have a distorted view of how our clients will perceive us if we actually start to offer positive services and the products that go with them.

It may sound as though I am reinforcing those who say that CPAs will never sell—far from it. I just think the first step in overcoming our resistance to selling is to admit that it is a problem, identify its cause, and then find a way to solve it. That's where TOPS comes in.

Most books and sales courses today focus on closing techniques and prospecting. When I read and attended these, I came away with ideas that I tried to put into practical use. However, I could never bring myself to ask a redundant question or to use any of the standard closing techniques. I didn't like to have them used on myself, so why should I use them on my clients? I didn't have an *ethical* problem with using them, because I felt that my clients needed to take the steps I was recommending. But I did have a *comfort* problem. I just couldn't do it. So I started using approaches that seemed comfortable to me. That's how I devised the following four parts to the sales presentation.

1. Trust

People will not buy from someone they do not trust. Fortunately for us CPAs, our clients already trust us. However, they may need a little reassurance in order to trust us in our new roles. In regular sales training, you would be told to spend a good deal of time observing the client's office, looking for things he or she might be interested in, such as sports, family, awards, and so on.

You will be seeing most of your clients in your office. Since you already have a good deal of information about your clients, you need not spend a great deal of time on typical questions to generate trust. For the CPA, these are just preliminaries. A typical trust question might be, "I noticed from your tax return that your income was up last year. Congratulations! How did you accomplish that?" This (1) tells the client that you are interested enough to notice, (2) reminds the client that you are his or her tax advisor and that you understand the client's financial situation, and (3) makes the client feel good. Another even lighter question to remind a client of your close relationship could be, "I noticed that Jane (his wife) went to work at the University last year. How does she like it?" Another, and tougher, question might be, "When do you plan on retiring?" This is also a good time to ask typical tax-planning questions. It solidifies the client's trust and shows that you are comfortable with the subject.

Remember to listen to the answers.   The purpose of this trust session is primarily to gather data and to get relaxed. Ideally, you should already have available one or more of these tools to help you:

1. A preliminary questionnaire indicating the areas in which the client needs help.
2. A goals sheet completed by the client.
3. The client's tax return.
4. A completed financial plan.

However, you can make it though the interview without any of these tools. They just make your chances of success much greater.

Don't linger too long, because if you do, your client will do one of two things:

1. If busy, the client will become fidgety and cut short the more important steps.
2. The client will get comfortable and start telling you stories so long that you will never get to steps 2, 3, and 4.

For a long-term client with whom you have a great relationship, spend only two minutes on trust questions. For others, you might want to ask as many as three questions to ease any possible tension.

2. Opportunity

The next questions to ask point out problems. The client has to be made aware of a problem he or she has. If this client doesn't have any financial problems, then you should be talking to another client. A typical question might be, ''Bob, your income last year put you in the top 10 percent of Americans in terms of earnings. However, I also notice that you don't have much saved. How much is your retirement plan at work going to provide when you retire?''

Listen.

You should already know the answer to this question. The typical retirement plan is going to pay in a range of 20 to 60 percent of current salary. Most fall in the lower range. You have now pointed out a problem. However, Bob may still consider it to be *your* problem, not his. After all, he didn't have it when he came into your office.

If your clients don't have the funds to warrant a long-term financial plan, don't you feel somewhat responsible? Who is their primary financial advisor, after all? If your client gives you this excuse, then I see a minimum of three opportunities.

1. Client needs an emergency fund—start a bank draft.
2. Client needs a goals funds—start a bank draft.
3. Client may need health, life, or disability insurance. He or she certainly can't afford any uninsured losses.

3. Pain

You must now personalize the problem by making the client uncomfortable. Don't worry, it's for his own good. You might ask, ''Bob, from what you tell me, your income could drop from $175,000 to $50,000 when you retire. Since you don't have much in the way of investments to add to your income, are you prepared for a 70 percent drop in your standard of living?''

Listen.

If this doesn't faze him, ask him another ''pain'' question: ''Yes, I understand that your mortgage will be paid off by the time you retire, but what do you think will happen to maintenance, insurance, and taxes during the next 10 years?''

Listen.

"That brings up the subject of inflation. What do you think the inflation rate will be for the next 10 years?"

Listen.

Pull out your financial calculator and calculate what his equivalent earnings will be 10 years into retirement: "If inflation does run at 4 percent during those 10 years, the value of your $50,000 will have decreased to $33,778. Do you feel comfortable with that type of income?"

Listen.

If Bob is not thoroughly upset by now, address some specific lifestyle questions, such as: "I see you on the golf course a lot, and I know that you love to travel. I also know that you enjoy driving a nice new Cadillac. I think that it is wonderful that we get to enjoy the fruits of our labors. As your financial advisor and friend, I see it as my obligation to do everything possible to help you to continue to enjoy what you have worked so hard for. But will you be able to keep up the membership in the club, drive Cadillacs, and travel on this fixed income? Which items are not all that important to you?"

Listen.

4. Solution

By this point you have:

1. Reinforced the trusting relationship that you enjoy with your client;
2. Pointed out a problem that he may have been only vaguely aware of or chose to ignore; and
3. Personalized the problem by making the client feel pain. He knows what may happen to him if he doesn't fix the problem. He should now recognize that it is *his* problem, not yours.

It's time for the knight in shining armor to arrive. You will ask some solution or comfort questions, such as: "How important is it to you to maintain or even improve your current lifestyle when you retire?"

Listen.

"Would you feel more secure about your future if you knew that you were going to be able to protect yourself against inflation?"

Listen.

"If there was a way to do this without severely affecting your current lifestyle, how important would that be to you?"

By this time, your client should be telling you the benefits he wants from retirement. Most clients will throw you at least one curve ball, such as: "I know I've got a problem, but my mortgage payments are so high because I do want the mortgage paid off when I retire. I also have two kids in college that are draining me. There is just not enough to go around."

Don't let him get away with this excuse. You just change tactics and say, "If I could show you a couple of adjustments you could make in your lifestyle that could possibly free up the funds you need to protect yourself from that 70 percent drop in living standard, how important would that be to you?" You have again reminded him of the pain and positioned yourself as the solution.

It's now time for the "close," but let's not use that word. It builds a wall in your mind. Your client should already have decided. All you have to do is present the solution: "Bob, as I see it, you could build a retirement fund of approximately $350,000 by investing only $2,000 per month in a couple of quality mutual funds. I don't know what the rate of return will be in the next 10 years, but I have used an assumed rate of 8 percent in my calculations. Although that $350,000 will not make up the shortfall in your retirement income completely, it may put you back on the golf course and throw in a little travel. The longer you wait, the more per month is going to be required, so I suggest that you start with the program today. I can get the paperwork done before you leave today. How does that sound?"

Stop talking. Listen.

It is critical that you do not speak before the client does at this time. Let the client answer.

The client should be ready for you to call in your assistant now. The assistant should take the client to another office to complete the applications. Notice that no product has been mentioned yet. When the paperwork is finished, your assistant will go over the product in detail with the client. You will step in at the very end and make sure that the client fully understands the product. Most clients are not product oriented, they buy on emotion. Your client has bought on emotion. The visit with your assistant as the paperwork is being completed will give him plenty of time to justify his decision, using logic. If the client wants to discuss the product further, by all means do so. Just don't ever let the product be the main element of the sale. The client's need or problem, his pain, and your comforting solution are the driving points of the sale. If you live by selling product and performance, you will also die on product and performance.

Too easy, you say? Maybe, but this is the way that 80 percent of my interviews go. It works if you believe in yourself and in what you are doing for your client. That belief will shine through any mistakes you make in presentation or objections your client may have.

For example, suppose that when presented with the $2,000 proposal, Bob had said, "Jim, I just told you that there is no money left. I'll just have to wait till the kids get out of college."

I would reply, "I understand completely. However, if you wait another four years, the $2,000 per month goes up by 89 percent to $3,778. The alternative is to pay the $2,000 for 6 years instead of 10. That will grow only to $185,000 (about half as much) using the same assumptions.

"What happens if your income goes down in the interim or you suffer some sort of health problem? Bob, I'm not going to presume to tell you which parts of your spending patterns you need to adjust, but we both know that you are spending more than 90 percent of the other people in the country. The best way I have found to budget is to save first. The rest will take care of itself. Let's start with $2,000, and then if you just can't stand it after a couple of months, call me and we can adjust. But let's not procrastinate in solving this problem."

Sample Questions Using TOPS

The following list illustrates samples of various TOPS questions:

Trust (Preliminary) Questions

Light preliminaries
1. "What is involved in your new job?"
2. "Looks as if you got stuck with $_____ interest expense last year that was not deductible. Did you know that personal interest is no longer deductible?"

Medium preliminaries
1. "When do you plan to retire?"
2. "What type of lifestyle do you envision for yourself when you do retire?"
3. "I noticed on your tax return that you have 100 percent of your money invested in CDs. Is there a reason for that?"
4. "You own stock in _____ company. Mind if I ask how you came to own it?"
5. "You have IRAs in at least four different places. May I ask how that came about?"
6. "_____ percent of your Social Security income was taxed last year. Are you comfortable with that?"
7. "I notice that you are not employing your children in your business even though they are old enough to work there. Are you aware of the benefits of doing this?" (This type of question may not get you any direct business, but it will be appreciated by your client and will establish trust.)

Most of the preceding questions are taken directly from the tax return. They are questions that your competition may not have access to or know how to use.

If the client has a goal sheet, just ask a couple of light questions from the sheet to break the ice. Save the best for the Opportunity and Pain steps.

1. "I notice you want to become financially independent at age 50. Is there a significance to that age?"
2. "Your Goal Sheet mentions travel. Are we talking about international travel?"

Opportunity (Problem) Questions

Tools to help you identify problems
1. Tax returns for this year and the prior year.
2. A post-tax interview questionnaire.
3. A preliminary inquiry sheet completed by the client indicating areas of interest in financial planning.
4. A goals sheet.

The tax returns and goals sheets are most important. You can, however, proceed without either.

1. "Mary, from your goals sheet, I see that educating your two children is very important to you. However, I have not been able to identify funds set aside for this purpose. Do you have any set aside?"
2. "Since educating your children is high on your goals list, what provisions have you made to ensure that they will be educated in the event that something happens to you or your husband?"
3. "You indicate that you would like to be financially independent at age 55. Can you identify the amount of income or assets that would meet your criteria for financial independence?"
4. "Schedule B shows that you own some individual taxable bonds. What are the rates on these bonds? When do they mature? Are you aware of the call provisions?"
5. "You own some tax-exempt bonds, yet you paid no taxes last year. Do you think that a taxable bond might get a better overall return?"
6. "Some portion of the funds you contributed to IRAs last year were nondeductible. Would you be interested in alternatives that allow more flexibility and less recordkeeping."

Pain (Personalized Problem) Questions

Remember, pain questions are used to *personalize* the problem surfacing through the opportunity questions you have already asked. Remember to listen to the answer and take notes after each question.

1. "Lisa, my calculations show that it will cost approximately $94,000 to educate Shawn and $118,000 to educate Courtney if they both attend the private university you attended. Are scholarships assured for either? Your income and assets make financial aid a little doubtful. Do you plan for them to work part-time?"

2. "If anything happened today to you or your husband, do you have alternative plans for educating the children? My calculations show that you need at least $150,000 in insurance to take care of the kids from now through college, and $250,000 for your husband. How much of your coverage is designated for this purpose?"

3. "You have indicated that you want to be financially independent at age 55, and you have defined that as having $250,000 in assets and $50,000 per year in income. You are 40 today, so that leaves us with 15 years to reach your goal. You have $50,000 saved toward your goal now. To reach your goal of $250,000, you will need to save $574 per month, starting now. However, in order to produce $50,000 per year in income, you will need approximately $800,000 in assets. Where did you plan to get the other assets or income? Do you have sources of income for retirement that do not show on your tax return?"

4. "The rates on your taxable bonds are high in relation to today's market conditions. If they are called, do you realize that your principal will be returned to you before maturity? What are your plans for reinvestment of this principal? Has the investment representative who sold them to you counseled you on call provisions? Is there a possible capital gain tax to be paid? Did your investment counselor advise you of the necessity of keeping track of your basis in the bonds?"

5. "Were you paying taxes when you bought the tax-exempt bonds? What was the taxable equivalent yield at that time? Would you like to compare this with a taxable bond's after-tax rate of return even if it causes you to pay some taxes?"

6. "Have you kept separate records for your deductible IRAs versus nondeductible IRAs? Are you aware of the necessity of annually reporting their status indefinitely? What was your primary purpose in contributing to the IRAs?"

Solution (Comfort) Questions

1. "What is important to you about having the children attend your alma mater? If they can attend a quality state school close to home, the estimated costs decrease to $47,000 for Shawn and $52,000 for Courtney. If you plan for this alternative, you can meet your goal by saving only $135 per month for Shawn and $120 per month for

Courtney. Could this be at least an interim solution until we get a firmer idea about which school they will attend?''

2. ''That takes care of the long-term problem of getting the kids educated, assuming you are able to save according to schedule. Would it be useful if I could weave the long-term savings program into your total plan and squeeze out enough money to insure against premature death or disability? After looking at your permanent coverage, I think you can purchase term insurance to cover your education funding needs for only $75 per month on both you and your husband. Does term insurance to cover this temporary need sound satisfactory to you?''

3. ''Unless you can come up with a substantial increase in income or inherit some assets, I don't think we can plan around a retirement at age 55 with the type of income you plan to have. Why is retiring young important to you? Would you be willing to compromise on the retirement dates if I can show you how you can meet your goals for income? My calculations show that you may need to work until age 62 when your company retirement kicks in. If it produces the $20,000 per year you estimate, we will need only $30,000 additional income. If you can save $625 per month starting now, you can reach your goal. We will need some additional principal to protect you against inflation, but does this sound like a good start toward your goals?''

4. ''If I can show you how to avoid the call provisions of your bond and increase the income you are currently earning, would you consider that a reasonable solution? My calculations show that you could sell your taxable bonds at a premium today and incur no tax liability. If you reinvest the proceeds in a mutual fund, you will increase the current income on the bond to more than you would receive if you wait until the call provisions take effect. If you agree, we can start the process of selling the bonds today.''

5. ''You made a good decision at the time you purchased your tax-exempt bond. However, you are currently paying no taxes. Does a better opportunity for growth in conjunction with the goals you stated to me sound OK? If you sell the bond today, you will incur no taxes. You can reinvest the proceeds in a growth fund to work toward your goal for retirement.''

6. ''You are making contributions to your nondeductible IRA in order to provide for your future retirement and to receive the benefit of deferred taxation on earnings. Which alternative sounds better—a tax-deferred investment that requires *no reporting* to the IRS each year with *no limit* on the amount you can contribute, or an investment that will grow but not have that growth subjected to tax until you sell it? Since you are not currently paying taxes, you may want to consider the growth investment.''

These questions are samples only; they have not been taken from actual cases nor subjected to accuracy tests. They are meant to show you the difference between trust (preliminary), opportunity (problem), pain (personalized problem), and solution (comfort) questions. Note that in all cases products are mentioned generically only. Remember that a person's buying is based on emotion, then later justified based on logic. These questions will pique the emotions and allow people to feel that they are in control, but that you are the vehicle they need to arrive at their goals.

A QUICK REFERENCE LIST FOR TOPS

Trust

Use trust questions to relax and establish rapport with your client. Use light preliminary questions about personal situations and medium preliminary questions to casually ask about goals. The purpose is to cement a trusting relationship with your client and to help him or her to see you as more than a tax advisor.

Opportunity

Use opportunity questions to point out problems that the client has in reaching her financial goals, reducing taxes, and so forth. You are going to try to get the client to think more clearly about her financial goals. Often, this may be the only time the client has ever given clear thought to where she wants to go financially. Most people go through life aimlessly without goals. Your job during the opportunity questioning is to ask questions that will get the client to open up to you and to see some problems that she may have. A good questioning technique in this step is to repeat the client's statements back to her; for example, "In other words, you want to retire early enough to enjoy some travel while your health is good."

Pain

This is where you make the client uncomfortable. Don't worry, it will be good for her. When you point out problems with questions, they are still *your* problems, not hers. When you personalize them by naming names and giving amounts, they become her problems. Use visual imagery, such as picturing the first child going off to the wrong college or going to work flipping burgers instead of going to college.

Solution

Now you can be the hero. Position yourself as the solution. Questions are not as important in this segment as solutions. This is where you make the sale. Your client should be feeling the problems emotionally, so she wants to get rid of the pain and find comfort. Give her the solution. Then be quiet!

OTHER TOPS TIPS

KISS (Keep It Simple Stupid, or Keep It Short and Simple)

Genius has been defined as the ability to reduce the complex to the simple. Don't use industry buzzwords. They just cause your client pain and make you the source of the pain, not the solution. Don't be afraid to present seventh-grade solutions to a Ph.D. He may know a lot about his field, but he may know nothing about yours. If he is very astute, you will pick this up early in the conversation and can adjust accordingly. Keep it short and simple.

Use Stories and Anecdotes

Particularly during the pain questions, throw in a story or two about cases you know of or have read about in which a client had a similar problem but failed to solve it. Add a story about a client whose problem was solved by you. Of course, you can't divulge client information, so you can use stories you have heard from other colleagues or read about. I have even used composite stories of various clients to emphasize my point. If a client has given me permission, I may even use names to emphasize success in the solution questioning phrase.

Try On Your Client's Shoes

Take note of everything about your client. For instance, is he a slow talker, nervous, high strung, laid back? What does his risk profile say? Try to get inside his head and think as he does. If you were your client, would this seem like a good deal? What would bother you about it? What would you want your financial advisor to say or do? Could you make a decision based on the facts given?

Tell the Client What to Do

Don't go overboard on the questioning, especially in the solution stage. Many sales trainers will tell you always to ask open-ended questions so that the client will give you feedback. However, there is a time to get some yes or no answers. That time is in the solution step. If you keep asking open-ended questions, both you and the client will tire of them. Most of my clients want me to tell them what to do. After all, you have positioned yourself as the trusted financial advisor. Now you must act like one.

Handling Objections

Clients often raise objections. The following paragraphs offer examples of objections, answers, and solutions.

The financial magazines I read say never to pay a load!

Solution 1. It is true that there is no conclusive evidence that load funds outperform no load funds over long periods of time. What is seldom mentioned is that the reverse is also true. There is no conclusive evidence that no load funds outperform load funds after all charges and fees over long periods of time. So what is the difference? The difference is my involvement.

Solution 2. Money magazine and financial writers for the business section of your daily newspaper seem to be engaged in a "feeding frenzy" when it comes to attacking products with commissions. Since the vast majority of these writers have never sold a product, prepared a financial plan, or worked one-on-one with a client the way that you and I are working today, it is their natural inclination to follow their predecessors in attacking commission-based products. The real facts are that all products (including financial products) must be marketed. Load funds are marketed primarily through people like me. No load funds are marketed through direct mail, television, and advertising in magazines and newspapers, such as the ones these writers work for. There is nothing wrong with either distribution system. If you can select your own funds, monitor them, and match them to your stated financial goals, then possibly the other distribution system is better for you. However, if you need help in doing these things, there should be no shame in buying load products.

Solution 3. I understand your concern about paying commissions. I always like to give my clients a choice of how they pay me. Most choose commission-based products because of the convenience. They also like the fact that they can call me about their investments at any time without receiving a bill. My rate is $_____ per hour, and I will be happy to work with you using no load products.

Solution 4. Thank you for bringing up the subject of commissions. I always make sure that my clients completely understand how I am compensated. Let's talk about the load versus no load issue. According to *Money* magazine and many others, this is a do-it-yourself world. I'm sure that the financial writers represent themselves in court, write their own wills. They would fill their own teeth if they could hold the mirror just right and use the proper tools. They never consult an architect when building a house. They never use a carpenter or plumber. After all, who can do the job better than you can do it yourself? I'll even bet they teach their own kids at home. Why bother using professionals? They seem to have relegated the job of financial planning to the complexity of filling potholes. If a person can prepare a financial plan, select products from thousands to implement that plan in accordance with age, risk profile, salary, job security, and special needs; monitor that plan and adjust it as circumstances change; then that person should certainly do his or her own financial planning.

Solution 5. It is true that many people of other professions are quite astute at selecting investments and monitoring their own financial progress. They have both the talent, knowledge, and time to do all the things necessary to reach their financial goals. However, I have found only a few of my clients who possess all of these attributes. Most need help. When you select no load funds, your financial advisor is your postman or a clerk in some city far away. When an emergency of any kind happens, such as a market crash or a major change in circumstances, most people need help. They have paid for that help with a commission.

Solution 6. Many people who purchased strictly no load funds could not reach their funds during the stock market crash of 1987. My clients could reach me.

Don't you have a conflict of interest when you sell a commission-based product?
Yes. Almost every delivery of a service has a built-in conflict of interest. Consider the thousands of lawsuits that shouldn't have been filed. How about the tonsillectomies, mastectomies, and ear tube operations that were unnecessary? From auto mechanics to audits, conflicts of interest are present. The question becomes one of *integrity.* Always select a financial advisor who wants to build a long-term relationship with you. Advising you to purchase the wrong product because it pays a fee will work in the short term, but not in the long term. Find someone you can trust and who has integrity. If you do not trust me, then I don't want you for a client.
Wouldn't the conflict of interest be solved by a fee-only planner?
Perhaps. There are many fine fee-only planners. I used to be one. However, there are many good products with loads that a fee-only planner may not be able to offer without rather delicate maneuvers in offsetting fees with commissions. Also, does a fee-only planner not trust his or her own integrity enough to deal with the conflict of interest issue? I don't have a problem with it, because I never select a product based on a commission. I select it based on my clients' needs. Finally, is there a conflict when a planner increases his or her fee without increasing his work?
I want to think it over.
When a client says this, one of two things has taken place:

1. You haven't been talking with the real decision maker.
2. You didn't make the pain severe enough.

If someone wants to think it over, I usually don't try to talk him or her out of it. Although I wish the client would make the decision then and there, I can appreciate the desire to "sleep on it."

Solution 1. I understand. This is a big step. Before you leave to make your decision, would you let me make some final notes to be sure that I will have everything ready when you give me your decision? (At this point, go back over your pain pointers to be sure that the client leaves feeling uncomfortable.)

Solution 2. No problem. We would not hold you to any decision made today, anyway. We always like to give our clients at least 24 hours to think about it. Since the plan is fresh on our minds now, however, would you mind going over the paperwork with my assistant so that we don't have to reinvent the wheel. You may even want to sign everything today under the condition that no action will take place until you give us a definite go-ahead.

Solution 3. That's perfectly understandable. Is there any particular concern that you would like me to go over before you leave? If there is a question later, please give me a call. Please bear in mind that some of the numbers and facts used in our projections are based on today's market conditions and that those can change rather quickly.

Solution 4. Certainly. May I just ask one favor? We think we have arrived at a solution that is as close to perfect as we can get for your needs. If you decide not to implement it, will you give me a call and let me know what you didn't like?

Selling When Your Client Insists on Talking Product

Most CPAs who get into this profession are sucked immediately into the product pit. I was no exception. When I wasn't frozen in nonaction because I couldn't decide on which was the perfect product, I was on an endless quest searching for the best product that had the lowest risk, highest return, and most flexibility of anything on the market. I tried to compete with the *Fortune* list, the *Money* magazine list, and so on.

There will be more about products later in this book, but for now remember this advice: select no more than two or three mutual fund families and insurance companies, and concentrate your business. You will do yourself, the product sponsors, and your clients a favor.

When your client wants to talk product, let her. I mean let *her* do most of the talking. Rephrase her questions and statements and feed them back to her or ask a question such as "Why is that important to you?" Let the client know early on that you are not trying to locate the world's greatest product because that is a foolish quest. Sooner or later, if you mostly keep quiet, the client will have to show that she doesn't know much about product. If she does, then you don't want to argue with her.

When the client settles down, describe the *perfect investment* on your grease board as follows:

1. Has a high yield and rate of return.
2. Has tax benefits.
3. Has no commission.
4. Has complete liquidity.
5. Has no risk.

"Ms. Client," you say, "the perfect investment does not exist. So which of these is most important to you?"

```
THE PERFECT INVESTMENT

• Has a high yield and rate of return.
• Has tax benefits.
• Has no commission.
• Has complete liquidity.
• Has no risk.
```

Never sell on yield alone!

I hate to hear the words, "What does yours pay?" I know it is going to be a long conversation. The answer, again, is to feed it back with a question such as, "What do you mean by *pay*?" Are we talking about yield, income distribution, cash on cash return, or internal rate of return? When your client can't answer that, then ask her what she is trying to accomplish with her investment. Does she want income or growth or both?

Closing Techniques

Selling isn't selling, it's asking! Never mind the future close, the Ben Franklin close, the puppy close, the small matter close, the balancing close, the authority close, the positive alternative, or the sense of loss. Use TOPS. Ask TOPS questions in the right places. Listen to the answers and take notes. When you have let the client get into an emotional state of pain, you simply take him or her to the point of comfort and pleasure by solving the problems and taking away the pain. In this phase, you simply say things like, "Does this solution seem sensible to you? If it does, I don't think we should delay any longer. We would like to prepare the paperwork today. My assistant needs to go over the details with you now." Call in your assistant, and congratulate the client on going forward.

A word of caution: At this point, don't keep selling pain. You'll talk yourself out of the sale.

2

Finding Your Niche: Designing a Marketing Plan

"Finding your niche" sounds a lot better than "designing a marketing plan." If I were reading a book and saw a title that said "Designing a Marketing Plan," *skimming* would be a gross exaggeration to describe my reading of the material within. That's because the words *planning* and *marketing* have had such a negative connotation for me. They translated into words and phrases such as *work, seldom used, wasted time,* and so forth. I think the reason is that I connect these terms to the academic world and huge corporations, where marketing plans are prepared by people who have never implemented one. When I learned to think of a marketing plan that would *save me work* and *make me money,* it became a working tool rather than just a huge report slightly above the rank of a policy and procedure manual. Also, the term *marketing* is broad. It was hard for me to get my arms around it. For example, I couldn't quite distinguish the difference between selling and marketing. I read somewhere that *selling* is getting a client to buy a product or service, whereas *marketing* is finding a client to sell to.

So how did I develop this change of attitude? Through the process of goal setting and attitude training. I also did it out of necessity. When I first began to discover the great opportunities awaiting me in the world of helping people get control of their financial lives, I was excited at the multitude of ways to make money by helping other people—but also overwhelmed. I couldn't decide which one to attack first and often found myself frozen by inaction. I knew something had to change, so I set aside two days away from work to develop a plan. When I decided to really make a plan rather than just talk about it, my subconscious began to send me messages of what should be in the plan. I started a list of areas in which I had interest, set up a folder, and began stuffing notes into it. By the scheduled time for ending my planning session, I had the rough outline of a plan in mind. Here's a summary of what worked for me:

1. Decide that a marketing plan is not a dust-gathering document, but a useful tool that will save you time and work, reduce your stress, and make you money by allowing you to serve more people.
2. Set aside at least one day, preferably two, when you will work away from the office to prepare the plan.
3. Set up a folder titled "Marketing Plan."
4. Write down all the topics and ideas that start coming to mind *when* they enter your conscious mind. These are messages from your subconscious. Take them seriously. Stuff the notes into your folder.
5. On the scheduled planning days, prepare a rough outline of your plan.

If you need help, see the sample list of opportunities that follows.

Master List
Major Marketing Opportunities

1. Retirement Plans and Planning
   a. 403(b)/ORP tax-sheltered accounts for employees of tax-exempt organizations that qualify under IRC 501(c)(3) (primarily schools and colleges).
   b. 457 plans for tax-exempt organizations that are not 501(c)(3)—primarily cities and counties.
   c. 401(k) and other qualified plans for non-tax-exempt organizations.
   d. Nonqualified plans and private pensions.
   e. IRAs.
   f. Simplified Employee Pension Plans and Salary Reduction Simplified Employee Pension Plans.
   g. Planning for early retirement, lump-sum distributions, etc.
2. Payroll Deduction Group Sales
   a. Savings by payroll deduction.
   b. Group health and disability.
   c. Group life.
3. Business Continuation Planning
   a. Buy-sell agreements.
   b. Employee Stock Ownership Plans.
   c. Business interruption and disability insurance.
   d. Business valuation for estate planning and business succession.
4. Cafeteria Plans
5. Traditional Insurance
   a. Life insurance marketing to individuals.
   b. Disability insurance for individuals.
   c. Insurance in business:
      • Split dollar.
      • Executive bonus.
      • Nonqualified retirement plans.
   d. Health insurance:
      • Individual health.
      • Medicare supplement.
   e. Long-term care insurance.
6. Estate Planning
   a. Wills, powers of attorney, living wills, living trusts, credit shelter trusts, life insurance trusts, etc.
   b. First to die, second to die, survivorship life insurance.
   c. Charitable giving.
7. Insurance as an Investment
   a. Annuities:
      • Fixed.
      • Variable.
   b. Variable life.
   c. Universal life.

8. Financial Planning from the Tax Return
   a. Post-tax interviews.
   b. Plans from the tax return.
   c. Off-season interviews.
9. Selling Financial Products Through Banks
10. Financial Counseling and Training Through Businesses
    a. Fee-based workshops.
    b. Executive financial plans.
11. Education Funding
12. Planning for the Elderly
13. Other Investment Products Marketing
    a. Mutual funds.
    b. Unit investment trusts.
    c. Individual securities.
    d. Others.

This isn't meant to be a complete list. There are dozens (probably hundreds) of marketing opportunities not included. You may want to concentrate on only one or two. My approach was to try to attack most of them because of the nature of my clientele. I knew that specialization would probably be more efficient and profitable if it would work, but I did not feel that specialization would work in the very small market I was in. I also wanted to practice the concept of holistic financial planning. I felt that this necessitated that I have a working knowledge of all areas of the financial and estate planning spectrum.

"Progress always involves risk; you can't steal second base and keep your foot on first."

—Frederick Wilcox

"First comes thought, then organization of that thought into ideas and plans; then transformation of those plans into reality. The beginning, as you will observe, is in your imagination."

—Napoleon Hill

CHOOSING YOUR PRIMARY AREAS

How, then, do you choose? Use the following steps in selecting among the major marketing opportunities you have identified.

1. Rate each category that appeals to you on a scale of 1 to 10. Appeal refers to level of interest and excitement generated by your thinking of the possibilities.
2. Rate each category as to your existing knowledge and experience on a scale of 1 to 10.

3. Rate each category as to the level of need that your present clients have for the service on a scale of 1 to 7.
4. Rate each category as to the level of need in your marketing area for the service on a scale of 1 to 5.

Total the score for each category. Concentrate your efforts as the total scores indicate. For example, the highest score possible for a category would be 32. If a particular category scores 25 or better, it's time to get on with the plan.

GOALS, ACTION, AND RESPONSIBILITY PLAN

After selecting the areas where you want to concentrate your efforts, you must do the following:

1. Develop specific action steps to implement your plan.
2. Define your target market (who needs this type of service?).
3. Use the rules of goal setting and time management, including delegation. Although a marketing plan should be developed even when you work alone, it is a much more effective tool when the responsibility is distributed appropriately with staff who share your goals.

See the action plan in Form 2.1.

Summary of Steps—Developing a Marketing Plan

1. Develop a master list of marketing opportunities. Samples and steps for developing the list have been discussed earlier.
2. Rate each opportunity, using the criteria provided.
3. Discuss the various categories listed with staff members, mentors, or others who may be able to provide guidance.
4. Set up a goals, action, and responsibility plan for each marketing opportunity.
   a. Decide who your target market is.
   b. Set your goals (the revenue you want to achieve for each target market, for example), with due dates.
   c. List the action steps necessary to reach your goals, with due dates for each step.
   d. Assign responsibility for each marketing opportunity and for each step.
   e. Input each major marketing opportunity as a project and each task under that project into your time management system.

Form 2.1   Sample Action Plan for a Marketing Opportunity

Current Update _____1993
Marketing Opportunity _____
Target Markets:

_____
_____
_____

Goals: 1. _____ Due Date _____
          2. _____ Due Date _____
          3. _____ Due Date _____

Steps Necessary to Achieve Goals (Arrange as close to sequential order as possible, although many steps may be going on simultaneously. Don't be afraid to go into detail, making the steps smaller bits of a large project.)

1. _____ Due Date _____ Proj. Assigned _____
2. _____ Due Date _____ Proj. Assigned _____
3. _____ Due Date _____ Proj. Assigned _____

What happens to the other marketing opportunities that didn't make the list of favorites? Keep them. We retain the original list as part of our marketing plan. It helps to sharpen our awareness of these opportunities. We may also list some activities that let us "test the water" for these areas to see whether they deserve more of our attention.

See the sample marketing plan in Form 2.2.

IMPLEMENTING A MARKETING PLAN

At this point, the hardest part of the work is over. If you have devoted the time and creative thought to determine the niche you are going to target, the goals you hope to achieve, and the steps necessary to meet these goals, then all you have to do now is to follow the steps listed next. You should "own" the plan. You should believe in it. The project and task management system will remind you if you meet or miss deadlines, but *belief* is what will make the plan work.

1. *Own* the plan. Believe in it.

Form 2.2 Sample Marketing Plan for the Nineties

Current update May 1992
Major Marketing Category 403(b) and ORP

Primary Responsibility   Leslie C. Killgore
Secondary Responsibility   Mary Lambert
Goals 1. Increase 403(b) clients by 25   Date 12/31/93
          (incr. sales by $5,000/mo. and comm. by $225/mo.)
       2. Increase ORP clients by 10   Date 12/31/93
          (incr. sales by $7,500/mo. and comm. by $300/mo.)
       3. Add 6 new schools to current active list   Date 12/31/93
       4. Get total monthly sales to $75,000 per month

Target Market: Faculty and staff of public and private schools in
               northeast Texas area within 100 miles radius of our
               office.

Steps Necessary to Achieve These Goals

1. Send letters to all current 403(b) and ORP clients advising of current balance, projection in 20 years, new products, and ask to increase. Also ask for referrals on P. S. Mary & LK—due 6/30/92.
2. Prepare referral letters for presentation when we increase—7/1/92.
3. Host a brunch/workshop at Greenville office for teachers at Bland,
   Greenville, Commerce, Cooper, Royce City, Caddo Mills, Sul-
   phur Springs, Campbell, Quinlan, Boles Home, and ETSU.
   Projects: Obtain lists of teachers from superintendents—LK—
   6/15/92.
   Send out flyer/invitation—MCC—7/5/92.
   Hold workshop—7/30/92.
4. Contact TSTA groups by mail for programs in school in fall or
   spring of next year—Mary—due 6/15/92.
5. Schedule appts. with junior colleges in area, including McKinney,
   Collin County, Mt. Pleasant, Paris, and Northlake in Irving—LK—
   due 7/15/92.
6. Call _____to see whether he can get us in schools. Get
   names of persons to see in each location—LK—9/1/92.
7. Follow up 8/15/92 for new personnel at _____—LK—due
   8/15/92.
8. Get list of all people retiring at _____. Send letter offering free financial consultation.
9. Schedule visit for one faculty/week about conversion to
   _____.

2. Be sure that each opportunity is put into your time management system as a project.

3. For each project, input all tasks with due dates.

4. Meet monthly at first to discuss and update the plan, and no less than quarterly thereafter. These meetings should be on everyone's calendar and should be assigned as tasks with due dates.

5. Revise the plan as necessary and no less often than semiannually.

6. Reward yourself and staff when goals are met and tasks are completed.

Remember that *activity* (doing the tasks) *will* lead to meeting the goals.

THE TOOLS OF A MARKETING PLAN

One of the many advantages of developing a marketing plan and assigning responsibility for completion of the tasks therein is the development of expertise within your staff. After my marketing plan was originally developed, I later enhanced it by adding a "responsibility chart."

As we began to implement our action steps, we discovered that they were generating a lot of business. Our problem then changed from one of marketing to selling and servicing. We saw the need to assign responsibility for various "tools" that were used in many different aspects of the marketing program. For example, the person implementing a 403(b) sale might uncover a need for a complete financial plan that was beyond the scope of his abilities. The natural inclination was to overlook that opportunity. To prevent this, we assigned responsibility for various areas of expertise or tools. If a prospect needed a complete financial plan, we would consult our responsibility chart and find the person who had primary responsibility for development of financial plans. That person would then develop the financial plan. Please don't discard this step because it sounds as though I am talking about a large staff. It was especially useful when I had a staff of 14 who worked on tax, audit, write up, and so forth, as well as in financial planning. However, this strategy is just as valuable with a staff of 3. The following is a list of some of the tools and areas of expertise we developed:

1. Individual and business financial plans.

2. Prospectuses and product material.

3. Seminars.

4. Portfolio monitor reports (periodic reports to clients on the status of their investments).

5. Newsletter and promotional mailings.

6. Media advertising.
7. Speaking engagements.

We added this list to our marketing plan and assigned a person to have primary responsibility for each tool or area of expertise. We also developed a "general" marketing category, which we used for items that did not fit readily into another category or applied to several categories. It included such things as writing general articles about the firm for the local press, obtaining premium prizes for gifts to clients, and so on.

Let's review the reasons for creating a marketing plan. A marketing plan:

1. *Gives you focus.* With several marketing opportunities available to you and the need to keep several other balls in the air at the same time, the natural tendency is to become unfocused. Often, we freeze into a state of inaction because there are just too many things to do. When your attitude improves, you want to get back to work on the opportunities, but you may have forgotten where you left off and you don't know where to start. A marketing plan helps you to refocus.

2. *Reduces stress.* When your mind can't recall all the good ideas you had, when you can't figure out where you are or who was supposed to do what, you can find relief by knowing that the marketing plan is your road map. Even if you get completely off track, you know that the plan clears the confusion.

3. *Saves time.* You don't have to keep reinventing the wheel. You just improve on the wheel already built and keep it rolling.

4. *Allows you to have confidence in staff.* The plan is a written guideline for members of your staff. They know what your goals are, what has to be done to reach the goals, who has to do what, and when it has to be done. You don't have to keep telling them.

5. *Develops expertise within your staff and yourself.* When you decide to focus on certain areas of a plan, you will improve your expertise accordingly.

3

Selling During Tax Season

"What? Are you kidding? You want me to do *something else* during tax season? You're nuts! You just don't understand my practice. You don't know what it's like around here between January 15 and April 30." These are typical comments from CPAs when I mention that they are not taking advantage of prime opportunities to sell their clients during tax season. I usually reply with these questions:

1. When do your clients come to see you without your even having to ask them?
2. When will your clients sit still long enough for you to discuss their financial status and plans for the future?
3. When do your clients treat your telephone calls as if they were as important as a call from the president?
4. When is your advice most sought and most revered?
5. When do you get your most inspirational ideas?
6. When is your adrenaline level at its peak, allowing you to give your best efforts to your clients?
7. When are you and your staff most efficient, approaching productivity levels of 500 percent above the rest of the year?

Unless your practice is different from mine, you will answer "tax season" to at least five of these questions. I would respond to all seven with that answer. I was in my third or fourth tax season when a revelation hit me. "I like this! I am pumped most of the time because of this great productivity, seeing clients, handling problems, giving advice." Once I realized that I was often at my best during tax season, I began to stop dreading it so much and actually to look forward to it.

In about the fifth or sixth year, I began to notice something else. I was getting some *great ideas* during this period of stimulation. However, even if I could remember them, I had a hard time following up on these ideas after tax season. Often, I would think, "Whatever made me think I could do that?" I continued to let the good ideas and the stimulation not expended on tax returns *go to waste*.

- Order—Let all your things have their places; let each part of your business have its time.
- Resolution—Resolve to perform what you ought; perform without fail what you resolve.
- Industry—Lose no time; be always employed in something useful; cut off all unnecessary actions.

(From Benjamin Franklin's *Thirteen Principles*)

When I started my practice, I didn't know what great odds were against me, but I did know that I would have to work exceptionally hard and continue to do things that would distinguish me from the competition. From the very start, I took extra time to do more than prepare returns. I discussed tax planning ideas and gave some general advice about saving for the future, managing money, education funding, and so on. My clients appreciated this attention, which did serve to set me apart. However, as the years went by, I was extremely disappointed to find that few clients ever actually acted on my advice about anything except taxes. They would invariably agree with what I was saying, but come back year after year with the same problems. A little cynicism about the value of my advice began to creep into my own mind. The strangest thing was that more people kept asking for advice on these matters. I had a three-pronged dilemma:

1. More clients were asking for my advice.
2. Except in tax matters, few were acting on my suggestions.
3. I was spending a lot of nonbillable time. Of course, the obvious solution is to bill. However, when the tax return is priced at the maximum the market will bear, how can you bill more—especially when you have encouraged clients to talk to you about nontax matters?

These developments were occurring simultaneously with changes in the tax law that took away most of the tools I had used for years in tax planning—another blow to the value of my advice. I decided to become licensed to sell investment products. During the first two years, I noticed several things happening:

1. I had a much greater closing percentage on sales presentations *during tax season*.
2. During tax seasons I had a lot of great ideas for clients, which were never implemented because:
   a. My clients would not come back to implement the ideas.
   b. I didn't follow up, owing to reluctance to call, off-season sluggishness, etc.
3. I was spending a great deal of time doing things that a clerk could do with software and other organizers.
4. I had many hot ideas for expansion of the financial planning practice during tax season, which we could never rekindle during the off-season.
5. Even though tax returns were still the best profit center for the firm, financial planning returned a lot more per hour for effort expended.

About the third year after becoming licensed, I evaluated every task performed during tax season, using these criteria:

1. Does the task require my level of expertise, or could someone at a much lower level do it—even if that person is not on staff presently?

2. What is the real return per time invested in this task as compared with financial planning?
3. Do I like doing this task?

I also evaluated every client interview with an eye toward efficiency, productivity, and enjoyment for the client and myself. I did not perform an efficiency study. This was an informal evaluation; notes were taken and lists were made. It did not take much of my time. Many of the notes were mental. My course became clear after that critical evaluation. I had to (1) severely cut back on pre-tax interviews, simple tax returns, unpleasant or long-winded clients and (2) start doing more postpreparation reviews and interviews. The next year, I designed the plan I share with you in this book.

The results of my new strategy were as follows:

- A 12 percent increase in tax revenues (the same level that we had been accomplishing in prior years).
- A 300 percent increase in income from financial planning and product sales.
- A learning period and a momentum that propelled my practice to levels of service never before achieved.

THE POST-TAX INTERVIEW SYSTEM

I was about to make a drastic change in my practice. I didn't know whether it would work. I considered it similar to the changes we made in 1981 when we decided to do tax returns in-house using a PC. Automating tax returns turned out to be worse than we could have possibly imagined. It seemed like a nightmare at the time, but it was what we had to do for the future of the firm. Compared with that, changing to post-tax interviews was a piece of cake. I spent the most profitable, productive, and stress-free tax season since I had been in the business.

In order to make such a drastic change, I knew that I would have to do some careful planning. Here is the plan I developed.

Pre-Tax Season

The following outline is helpful for planning pre-tax season activities:

1. During the off-season, have staff members prepare a Financial Planning Cover Sheet for each tax client. See Form 3.1. They are to fill in only the name and indicate whether the client is an existing investment client.
2. During breaks in work or at your leisure, complete the cover sheets, using your knowledge of the clients. I found that I could complete the forms for 98 percent of my clients without pulling the files. If you have clients whom you don't know well, you may have to enlist a staff member who knows the clients to assist you. The cover sheet is used for:
   a. *Rating* the client as to investment or financial planning potential.

Form 3.1   Sample Financial Planning Cover Sheet

Post-Interview Date _____

FINANCIAL PLANNING COVER SHEET FOR TAX RETURN

Client _____ Existing Investment Client _____
Date _____

1. Pre-interview by: Partner_____ Staff_____
2. This client will need:
   A. _____No Post-Appointment _____Ask Client _____Urge Client
   B. _____Goals/Investment Philosophy—Temperament (Include
                     Prudent Investor piece)
   C. _____Planning from the Tax Return
           To Be Prepared by   _____Preparer
                               _____Financial Planner—Ptr.
                               _____Financial Planner—Staff

   D. _____Data Gathering

	FIN.PLNG. PRE-PARER	FIN.PLNG. PTR.	STAFF
_____Entire Package	_____	_____	_____
_____Financial Data	_____	_____	_____
_____Income/Expense	_____	_____	_____
_____Policy Listing	_____	_____	_____
_____Estate Planning	_____	_____	_____
_____Advisor/Document Listing	_____	_____	_____

   E. _____Social Security Benefit Report or Completed Application
   F. _____Investment/Financial Plan Modules
           _____Basic
           _____Advanced (Use Check Sheet)
   G. _____Client Investment Performance Report
   H. _____Post-Interview Form—To Be Prepared by _____Ptr.
                                                 _____Staff
           Note: Post-Interview Package Will Include Each Item
           Checked Above.
   I. _____Other _____

b. *Rerouting* clients who are not profitable, enjoyable, or necessary for you to see in order to prepare the tax return.

c. Providing all staff members, including your receptionist, with *directions* as to what is to be done for the client.

d. Ensuring that you are fully *prepared* before tax season, and before the client's visit to your office, with all the necessary information to properly present all the services you have to offer.

Line-by-Line Instructions for the Cover Sheet

Line 1: Tells staff who will do the pre-interview.

Line 2: Lists all the information you will need before the client sees you after his or her return is prepared.

A. Post-Appointment or Not?

Instructions as to whether a post-appointment is needed and whether the client should be urged to set up an appointment. I recommend simply setting up an appointment after the return is prepared for all high-potential clients. Don't ask *before* the return is done. Just have receptionist call and set one up *after* it is prepared.

B. Goals/Investment Philosophy—Temperament

I recommend that these forms be completed for all clients, whether you see them or not. It is my opinion that you need this basic information before you can even begin a basic conversation about investments or planning.

C. Planning from the Tax Return

This form is to be completed after the return is prepared. See Form 3.2. It is designed to allow staff to identify potential financial planning needs from entries on the tax return. I usually have staff highlight high-potential items. The cover sheet allows you to give instructions as to whether you are going to complete this form or you want someone else to.

D. Data Gathering

Data-gathering packages are discussed in more detail in Chapter 5. These are usually prepared when you see a definite need for a financial plan to be prepared for a client. If you can catch the client during tax season, it is an excellent time to get as much information as possible.

E. Social Security Benefit Report

We regularly ask our clients to complete a Social Security Benefits Report form. A standard cover letter alerts the clients to the inadequacies of Social Security and positions you as the person who is thinking about their retirement. This letter and the report from Social Security stimulates clients to begin thinking about retirement. See Forms 3.3 and 3.4.

Form 3.2 Financial Planning from the Tax Return

Name(s) _____ Age _____ Date _____

_____ Age _____

(Please highlight priority items.)

1040 LINE REFERENCE		(X)	(X)

6c	DEPENDENTS
	1. Clients have pre-college-age children
	2. Need Form SS-5 for dependent Social Security Number
	Recommend:
	    A. Adequate Life Insurance
	    B. Adequate Disability
	    C. College Funding Plan		

7	WAGES
	1. Highly Paid? (Above $40,000 Single)
	                 (Above $50,000 MFJ)
	Recommend:
	    A. Salary Deferral Options
	    B. Charitable Giving
	2. Owner or Part Owner of Business?
	Recommend:
	    A. Salary Reduction Plans—
	       401(k), SAR–SEP
	    B. Key Person Insurance
	    C. Split Dollar
	    D. Disability
	    E. Buy–Sell Agreement
	    F. 80% Dividend Exclusion
	3. Employee of Tax-Exempt Organization?
	Recommend:
	    403(b)
	4. Employee of State or Local Government?
	Recommend:
	    457		

8a	TAXABLE INTEREST AMOUNT
	Client has CDs
	Client has individual bonds
	Client has mutual funds
	Client has low-yielding bank savings or MMA
	Recommend:
	    A. CD Roll-Over Program
	    B. CD Rate-Finder Service
	    C. Change of Broker/Dealer
	    E. High Yield MMA
	    F. Start Monthly Savings Plan		

Form 3.2 *(Continued)*

1040 LINE REFERENCE		(X)	(X)

	G. If High Tax Bracket:
	      Tax Exempts
	      Tax Deferreds
	Comments _____		

8b	TAX-EXEMPT INTEREST
	  AMOUNT
	Taxable equivalent yield
	  Recommend:
	    A. UITs, Mutual Funds vs.
	        Individual
	    B. Switch to Taxable If After Tax
	        Return Is Higher		

9	DIVIDEND INCOME
	  Recommend:
	    A. Value Line Analysis
	    B. Discount Brokerage
	    C. Diversification Plan
	    D. Mutual Funds
	    E. Higher Income Investments		

12, 18, 19	BUSINESS INCOME, WORKING
	  PARTNERSHIP, OR FARM
	  Recommend:
	    Retirement Plan		

13	CAPITAL GAINS OR LOSSES
	Unused capital loss
	  Recommend:
	    Sales of Capital Gain Investments
	    to Offset
	Capital gains:
	  Recommend:
	    Reinvestment of Proceeds		

16a	IRA DISTRIBUTIONS
	  Recommend:
	    A. Plan to Avoid Premature
	        Distributions
	    B. Consolidation to Avoid
	        Complexity of Mandatory
	        Distribution		

17a	PENSIONS AND ANNUITIES
	  Recommend
	    A. Roll-Over to IRA
	    B. Lump Sum Distribution
	        Analysis		

(Continued)

Form 3.2   (*Continued*)

1040 LINE REFERENCE		(X)	(X)
21a and b	SOCIAL SECURITY BENEFITS Recommend: A. Single Premium Whole or Universal Life to Avoid Tax B. Annuities to Avoid Tax		
24, 25	IRA DEDUCTION Nondeductible IRA Recommend: A. Tax Deferred Annuities B. Our IRA Products Transfer C. Contribution for This Year D. Early Contribution Next Year (Bank Draft)		
27	CLIENT HAS SEP OR KEOGH CLIENT QUALIFIES BUT HAS NO PLAN Recommend: A. Our Third-Party Administrator B. SEP C. Proposal from Mutual Fund D. Transfer of Assets		
Schedule A	NONDEDUCTIBLE INTEREST PAID Recommend: Budget Planning/Savings Program CHARITABLE GIFTS A. Charitable Remainder Trusts B. Contribution of Appreciated Assets OTHER SPECIAL CONSIDERATIONS _____ _____ _____ _____		

**Form 3.3   Sample Letter to Clients—Adding Financial Planning
and Post-Tax Interview**

Dear Client:

We are pleased to announce a series of new services available from our firm, as well as some changes to our prior methods of delivering services. We think you will like the additional services you are going to receive. Don't worry, if you are happy with the way things have been done in the past and don't want any changes, we are flexible enough to continue our services just as before for all clients who request it. We know that most of you will want to take advantage of the changes we have implemented.

We have more computer power in our offices than we could possibly have dreamed of only a few years ago. Combined with tax law changes, sophisticated software and hardware have shifted tax return emphasis away from the interview *prior* to preparing the return to the need for an interview *after* the return is prepared. There is now more need to plan for *next* year and the future than to talk about what happened last year. Accordingly, I will be spending some time with you after your return is prepared this year. There is no extra charge for this service.

Changes in tax laws, an ever-changing global economy, and requests from clients make it necessary for any forward-thinking financial services firm to adapt quickly in order to meet client needs. We know that it is no longer adequate just to prepare tax returns. Clients need assistance not only in lowering taxes, but in reaching financial goals of a secure retirement, educating children and grandchildren, and investing wisely.

I am now a Registered Representative of 1st Global Capital Corp. This affiliation allows me to provide the assistance that my clients need and demand. What do we need from you in order to provide these expanded services? A little of your time and some information. We look forward to seeing you soon. Please call me if you would like to discuss our new services.

Sincerely,

_____

Form 3.4   Sample Social Security Benefits Letter

Dear _____

I have enclosed your Social Security benefits estimate. In summary, it shows the following:

1. Estimated monthly income to you at age 65.
2. Estimated monthly income to you at age 66 (normal retirement age).
3. If you die, your family would receive on approximate monthly income of $_____ .
4. If you become disabled, your monthly income would be approximately $_____ .

(You should be aware that Social Security disability benefits require *total* and *permanent* disability. You are highly unlikely to ever collect this benefit. You are very likely to become *partially* or *temporarily* disabled before retirement age.)

Questions you should ask yourself:

1. Can you maintain or improve your standard of living on this level of Social Security benefits?
2. What are you doing to keep yourself from being totally dependent on Social Security? Is what you're doing enough?
3. Are you covered for your biggest risk—*disability*?
4. Is your family protected if you die or become disabled?

Stop worrying about it and *do* something about it! We can help. Why not take advantage of our free professionally qualified assistance? Phone our office today for an appointment to go over this in person.

Sincerely,

_____

F. Investment/Financial Plan Modules

If we are fairly certain that we will be preparing a financial plan for a client, then I may ask staff to pull the forms necessary to do the plan. The *basic* package includes forms required to do a very basic or short plan. If an advanced plan is anticipated, I use the *module directory* to check off the forms I need. Module packages for preparing financial plans are provided in the expanded *Financial Planning: The CPA's Practice Guide.* This part of the cover sheet was useful for me because I worked on plans in a variety of locations, including my home office and one of our branch offices. When I was away from available forms, it was very convenient to know that the forms were already with the file. This is also an excellent way to save time. You shouldn't be using your time to pull forms.

G. Client Investment Performance Report

For clients who already have funds invested with you, it is wise to have a performance report available on those investments and to be prepared to discuss and reaffirm the quality of the decision that the client made. This can also lead to more sales.

H. Post-Interview Form

This form is simply a series of TOPS questions to ask the client. (See Form 3.6 on page 48.) I usually use a few points in the tax return or supporting data to reestablish trust and to get the client comfortable with what we are going to talk about. Then I ask a few opportunity questions about reducing taxes for next year and problems I noted from last year. Most of the other questions are pain questions, whereby I personalize the problems found, affirm my good intentions and desire to help as the reasons for causing the pain, then offer a solution. This may lead to getting the client's permission to help him or her solve those problems, a completed sale, or permission to proceed with a complete financial plan. *At the very least, it will reposition you as more than just a tax preparer.*

3. After the cover sheets are checked as required for each client, they are placed on top of the client's tax file.
4. Prior to tax season, you may want to advise your clients of changes you have made in your practice to adjust to changes in tax laws and in the economy, and in response to client requests.
   a. Send each client a letter with general information about your new services and how they can be beneficial to the client.
   b. You may want to consider making a video of yourself explaining the changes. It can be played in the reception room for clients while they wait. Response to this presentation was excellent in our firm.
   c. Train your staff thoroughly about how to handle the new procedure. A sample of our internal procedure and instructions to staff is shown in Form 3.5.

Implementing this procedure should free up about 60 percent of your time during tax season to do financial planning. Who absorbs that 60 percent? In most cases, including ours, it was absorbed by staff who had previously been performing well beneath their capabilities. Most were pleased with the new opportunities for client interaction.

Form 3.5   Sample Procedure and Instructions Memo

To: Policy and Procedure Manual
Route to: All Staff
Subject: Financial Planning and Tax Returns
Date: _____

Our Goals

1. Obtain basic data-gathering package for each client.
   a. Goals/Investment Philosophy—temperament.
   b. Financial data.
   c. Insurance policy listing.
2. For high-potential clients—all financial data.
3. Put together post-interview packages for partners or financial planning staff for each client.
4. Post-interview all clients.

Our Tools

1. Planning from the tax return.
2. Data-gathering packages.
3. Asset allocation software.
4. Post-interview questionnaire.
5. Financial/investment planning modules.
6. Social Security benefits report.
7. Investment performance reports.
8. Financial planning software.

Tax Department will produce a list of all tax clients. For each client, a Financial Planning Cover Sheet will be forwarded to the partner in charge or to a financial planning assistant.

Partner or Assistant will identify items required of each client by checking appropriate boxes.

All Staff with Client Contact

1. Emphasize the difference between the pre-interview for tax and the planning interview to discuss ways to solve client tax problems and meet client financial needs.
2. Try to set up each client with both pre-tax and post-tax appointments.
3. Emphasize the post-tax (planning) interview only if client wants one.

(Continued)

Form 3.5 (*Continued*)

---

4. Partner will do pre-interview *only if client insists*.
5. Refer to cover sheet to determine what information is to be gathered for the client.
6. During the pre-interview:
   a. Refer to cover sheet and gather data as required.
   b. Give client letter and request for data to bring to planning meeting.
   c. Ask for assistance from financial planning department if needed.
7. If no pre-interview, make request to client for data to bring to post-interview.
8. After return is prepared:
   a. Complete Planning from the Tax Return form (preparer).
   b. Investment performance report (fin. plng. staff) (for existing investment client).
   c. Other items required for post-interview as indicated on cover sheet. *Note:* Some items to be prepared by financial planner will be done during post-interview.
   d. Partner will (1) use "post-package" and prepare post-interview questionnaire in preparation for meeting with client; (2) complete financial plan if required.

Emphasize

1. That complete financial plans are available free of charge.
2. That there is never any cost for the post-interview.
3. The need for *total* financial planning.

Special handling for existing personal financial planning or investment clients should be noted on the cover sheet.

(Partner signature)

During Tax Season

The following paragraphs can be helpful in planning your strategy during tax season:

1. When clients come in, your staff should greet them and direct them in accordance with your instructions on the cover sheet and the written procedure. Staff should know the story by heart. Remember that even

though *other staff* will be doing the pre-interview, that *you* will visit with each client after the return is prepared. If you have a video, play it for clients. Keep copies of your letter announcing the changes to refresh their memories (unnecessary for clients who simply drop off or mail their tax data).

2. Ask each client to review and complete the goals sheet and risk profile questionnaires. I usually had the receptionist perform this step, but occasionally the tax preparer would do it.

3. If there is a pre-interview, have the preparer gather as much data as possible in accordance with instructions on the cover sheet. You are primarily looking for financial data, goals, and risk tolerance. Remember— most of the financial data will be available from the tax return data, so conducting an in-depth interview with the client is not necessary at this stage.

Sample questioning technique: "I see from your 1099 that you had interest income from Bank X. When Jim goes over your return with you later, he will want to know some additional information about your entire financial situation so that he can advise you properly. May I ask you some more information now about these investments and other matters so that we can have it ready for him to do an in-depth review of your tax return and its relation to your financial goals?"

If there is no pre-interview, the receptionist must be responsible for gathering the basics from the client when he or she drops it off. If it is mailed in, then the interview can be conducted over the phone.

The important thing is to be sure that as much information as possible is obtained. *This is not an audit. Don't expect to get exact figures.* In many cases, values of client accounts have been estimated based on interest income shown on the 1099s. The client will correct you if you use the wrong amounts. That is a good way to get the information you need.

4. After staff has prepared the return, it should be returned to you for final review, along with most of the information requested on the cover sheet. If some information is missing, that is OK. Complete data is not necessary to start the process, just very nice to have.

If a Financial Planning from the Tax Return form was completed, your staff has already highlighted the areas to review. If not, then this could be a good place to start. I have found that this form and the post-tax interview are excellent means of reviewing the return for *accuracy, completeness* and *tax planning*. You will uncover many ideas for reducing taxes in future years, as well as possible ways to prepare the return differently in order to reduce taxes for this year.

Using the forms, tax return, and data gathered by your staff, you can go over opportunities already evident and discover many more. I have never found a tax return that couldn't generate at least one opportunity question. Using the post-tax interview as your lead, highlight all of the *trust* (status), *opportunity* (problem), and *pain* (personalization of the problems) items you can find on the form itself.

5. After you are satisfied that the return has been completed correctly, have the staff process the return for pickup by the client.

(If you have uncovered opportunities in the return that warrant the preparation of a plan, then you can prepare the plan prior to seeing the client. This could be a mini-plan or a full-blown plan. I prepare mostly mini-plans during tax season. If the plan calls for action on investments, I have applications ready for the client's visit.)

6. When the return is ready for delivery, your receptionist should call the client, advise that his or her return is ready to be discussed with you, and set an appointment to do so.

7. When the client comes in, have the receptionist present the return and the bill to the client according to your normal procedure.

8. Take the client into your office for the post-tax interview. Have a copy of his or her return ready to go over. I usually have my copy marked in red ink on the lines I want to emphasize.

(Form 3.6 is a helpful guide in conducting the post-tax interview.) Be sure to use TOPS, as described in Chapter 1. The post-tax interview is perfect for its application. If all goes according to plan, the client should be in your assistant's office signing implementation paperwork after the interview.

FOLLOWING UP ON LEADS DEVELOPED DURING TAX SEASON

It is likely that you will develop all sorts of projects and leads during tax season. As hard as I tried to strike when the iron was hot, circumstances often prevented me from closing at that time. Perhaps a client had just renewed a CD, or was leaving on a trip and wanted to discuss it when she returned, or some other situation intervened.

I used to let a lot of these leads get away from me because I didn't have an efficient follow-up system.

The time and project management system helped to alleviate this problem, but adding financial planning and investments to my practice brought the problem roaring back. There was not room on my time and project management system to put all the notes I needed to remember to adequately follow up with this client. Moreover, each financial planning or investment prospect usually generated *several tasks*. When I did manage to get tasks assigned, I couldn't recall all of the *ideas* I had had during the initial discussions. As you know, I have a natural aversion to reinventing the wheel, so I often would not follow up at all.

Form 3.6   Post-Tax Interview
(Opportunity and Pain Questions)

Date _____

Name(s) _____   Age _____
         _____   Age _____

HIGHLIGHT EACH ITEM REQUIRING SPECIAL ATTENTION

1. Year_____   Tax Expense_____
   Too High_____
   About Right_____
   Reduction Techniques: 403(b) ____ 457 ____ 401(k) ____ IRA ____
                          SEP _____ Other Retirement Plan _____
                          Tax Deferred _____ Tax Exempts _____
                          LTD P/S _____ Other _____
                          _____

2. You lost $_____ in interest deductions last year.
   (Can you start paying cash?)
3. What are your plans for your refund? $_____
4. If you own a business, are you employing your children?
5. Are you mixing nondeductible with deductible IRAs?
6. Investment Income

		Yield	Est. Value
Interest—Taxable	$_____	_____	$_____
Interest—Nontaxable	$_____	_____	$_____
Dividends	$_____	_____	$_____
TOTAL	$_____		$_____

   Does this meet emergency fund needs? _____
   Is this your only source of retirement? _____
   It will generate about $_____ per month. Can you live on
   that?
   Is it in low-yielding accounts?   Rate? _____%
   It is increasing or decreasing each year?
   Do you know about the four treasure chests?
   - Emergency chest (3–6 months take home)
   - Recurring (nonemergency) expense fund
   - Midrange goals (education, house, investments)
   - Long-term goals and retirement
7. Are investments too concentrated?

Form 3.6 *(Continued)*

8. Are you doing excessive trading, trying to outguess the market?
9. What are your financial goals?
10. Your net worth is $_____. Your target net worth should be $_____ at age _____.
11. What are your plans for educating:

    Name_____Age_____Est. Costs $_____
    Name_____Age_____Est. Costs $_____
    Name_____Age_____Est. Costs $_____

12. You have several scattered IRAs. Are you aware of mandatory distribution rules at age 70-1/2? Consider consolidation. Are you paying fees on each one?
13. When do you plan to retire? Age_____ Years_____
    What percentage of your current income will you require at retirement? _____%
    Current income $_____ × _____% = $_____
    Years to retirement_____
    Income in future dollars $_____
    How much will your company pension plan pay? $_____
    How much will your IRAs and other
    retirement funds pay? $_____
    Today's GAP $_____
    Annual contribution $_____ for _____years.
    How much Social Security do you expect? $_____
    TOTAL BALANCE $_____
    (Where is this going to come from?)
14. You are four times more likely to become disabled for some period than you are to die before you retire.
    What would your family live on if you are disabled?
    What would pay for your children's education?
    We calculated your income continuation coverage requirement to be $_____. How much do you have?
15. We calculated your life insurance need at:
    Husband _____ Wife _____
    How much do you have?
    Is any of it permanent?
    What happens if you have a health problem and become uninsurable?
    What happens if you change jobs?

(Continued)

16. The life insurance industry has completely changed during the last 10 years.
    Do you have policies more than 5 years old? They may be antiquated and no longer fill the purpose. Do you know why you bought them?
    Will they be taxable in your estate?
17. Do you know that long-term care is not paid for by Medicare?
    Are you interested in filling this gap in coverage?
    You can protect $_____ in assets for only _____per month.
    Do you have parents who may need this coverage?
    If they have substantial assets, you may want to protect your inheritance or keep one of your parents from becoming destitute if the other requires long-term care.
18. Do you or your parents need Medicare supplement insurance?
19. How much are you paying for your health insurance?
20. If you own all or part of a closely held business:
    Do you have a plan for disposition?
    Do you have buy-sell agreements with partners/shareholders/family?
    Do you need help in selling?
    Have you considered ways to avoid capital gains tax when you do sell?

    Charitable Remainder Trust   _____
    ESOP and CRTs   _____

    Do you have overhead protection so that if something happens to you or your partner, your business can keep going?
21. We estimated your estate to be worth:
    $_____ today; $_____ in 10 years.
    We estimated your estate *taxes* to be:
    $_____ today; $_____ in 10 years.
    Do you want to "will" this much money to the IRS or would you rather your heirs or charity have it?
    Will there be enough "money" in your estate to pay these taxes?
    If your life insurance going to add to these problems?
22. Do you have a will?
    Did you know that probate could cost your heirs or you $_____.
    Did you know that a will is public information?
    Did you know that probate can take up to two years?
    Did you know that wills are valid only when you *die*?
    What happens to your assets if you are disabled?
    Whom do you think a court would appoint as your guardian?

Form 3.6   *(Continued)*

23. Do you have a living will?
24. Do you have a durable power of attorney?
25. Are you pleased with our services?
26. Would you recommend us to friends?
27. Would you sign a letter of introduction?
28. Names of friends and associates you believe could benefit from our services. (Give form if client wants time to think.)

    (1) Name _____

          Address _____

          _____

          Phone _____

    (2) Name _____

          Address _____

          _____

          Phone _____

Summary of Recommendations:

1. _____
2. _____
3. _____
4. _____
5. _____

Preparer's Comments:

_____
_____
_____
_____
_____

I solved this problem with the Investment Prospect Report. See Form 3.7. Using this form, I can make all the notes I need regarding discussions with the client, tasks that have to be assigned, products mentioned, and so on. This form is used to trigger entry of tasks into the time management system for the project in behalf of a particular client. This form itself is placed in the client's investment file. When the time management system reminds me that it is time for follow-up, *I can pull the file and review everything that was discussed.* That makes me a lot smarter when I confer with my client, who is usually impressed by my thoroughness.

Many of you have computer systems that can provide the same capabilities as this form. However, I have retained the Investment Prospect Report form and use it profitably.

Form 3.7   Sample Investment Prospect Report

INVESTMENT PROSPECT REPORT

Prepared by: _____
Date: _____
Rating: _____
(Hot, warm, good)

Client: _____
Date Contacted: _____
Method of Contact: _____
Route to: _____
Summary of Discussion: _____
_____
_____
_____

	Action Steps	Product	Resp.	Due Date	Task Assigned
1.	_____	_____	_____	_____	_____
	_____	_____	_____	_____	_____
2.	_____	_____	_____	_____	_____
	_____	_____	_____	_____	_____
3.	_____	_____	_____	_____	_____
	_____	_____	_____	_____	_____
4.	_____	_____	_____	_____	_____
	_____	_____	_____	_____	_____
5.	_____	_____	_____	_____	_____
	_____	_____	_____	_____	_____

4

In the Office

PHYSICAL OFFICE ARRANGEMENT

All of us have certain limitations on how we can arrange our offices. Don't let this stop you from making the most of what you have. My firm began as a store-front operation with everyone in one office. We later moved to a new location with three offices. When we outgrew that, we had people working next to the copy machine and in places where they had to move in order to get a door open. I say this in order to tell you that I understand about space limitations. The following are hints I learned from personal experience and training I received from others.

Desk or Table

Never put a desk between you and your client if you can avoid it. I prefer a small round or oblong table. If you are sitting with a husband and wife, try to sit between them so that both can see what you are presenting.

The Grease Board

Everyone should have a grease board (or other type of board) or a flip chart in his or her office to write on. This is an invaluable tool in selling. Most people are visual learners. They need to see illustrated what you are talking about. I also use the board to write down points or objections that my clients raise. I can then go back to those points to be sure that we have covered them all.

The Lobby

A lobby should reflect how you want your firm to be perceived by your clients. It should be tastefully decorated with good quality, conservative furniture. Preferably, clients should not be able to see or hear other parts of your office from the lobby. Never discuss client business in the lobby if you have any other private area at all. Even more important, never discuss one client's affairs in front of another.

If you have space for a client conference room, I highly recommend using it for all client discussions that don't take place in a private office.

If you display investment material in the lobby, it should be limited to pieces that reflect the image you want to create. I believe it is appropriate and profitable to use such material to spark client interest, but don't clutter the space so that the client is confused.

We maintain a bulletin board in our lobby, titled "News About Our Clients," where we post newsletters and media pieces featuring our clients. I also recommend an announcement board, welcoming all clients who are coming in that day. If you have sufficient space in your lobby, include a television set to play investment videos and messages or news channels.

Displaying Marketing Material

For some reason, displaying marketing materials was a big issue with me when I first entered the business. I desperately wanted something to show that I was a Registered Representative and that I could sell investment products. I later learned that the display is not nearly as important as TOPS. However, I believe that everything counts and the smallest matter can make a great difference. Displaying marketing material well may not make a lot of sales for you, but displaying it poorly or not at all may lose some.

Be sure that all prospectuses, annual reports, and so on are current. Outdated rates and prospectuses not only make you look bad, but could be illegal.

Keep a rate board in your lobby showing current rates for your favorite tax-exempt fund, local CD rates, brokered CD rates, annuity rates, and so forth. Be sure to use rates for products only in which yields are actually relevant. I seldom use them for products in which principal fluctuates. This is a very effective sales tool, however, because everyone identifies with CD rates. A rate board lets your clients know you are in the business better than any single display item I know of.

Charts showing stock market indices, the history of interest rates, and other pertinent items are interesting and, again, reinforce what you are doing in your clients' eyes. They won't make sales directly, but they pique interest.

We have tried all methods of storing the volumes of materials professionals receive from product sponsors. In the beginning, you will be concerned because you can't get needed information, but you will later worry about controlling the constant flow of materials. The best rule of thumb for prospectuses, annual reports, applications, and so on is to keep them in your plain sight, but not necessarily in the sight of your client. Open shelves work best. Enclosed files are cumbersome.

GREETING YOUR CLIENTS

I prefer to have clients announced to me over the phone intercom. I think it is best to leave your office and greet the clients personally in the reception area, rather than having them ushered back to see you. When you do greet them, be sure that you make physical contact in some way. A good firm handshake with both husband and wife is appropriate. I also highly recommend a friendly pat on the back for the man and, possibly, a light touch on the forearm of the woman. The extent of your cordiality depends on the type of relationship you have with the client, of course. You should never invade his or her "space" for too long, and all touches should be within the bounds of good taste.

As a conservative accountant, I was skeptical about the value of "touching,'' as advocated by the experts. However, I did start to notice successful people using it on others and on me. It works. You have to be sincere when doing it or it will appear contrived. This "establishment of contact" helped me to establish instant rapport with my clients and to feel closer to them. I was able to get to my opportunity and pain questions (see TOPS in Chapter 1) more quickly, because I emphasized the genuine concern I felt about my client's financial future.

Call clients by their names and instruct staff to do likewise. Think of how it makes you feel, when you walk into another person's place of business, to hear the sound of your name being called out in a friendly manner. You feel important and welcome. We had a rule that a client's name should be mentioned at least three times during every visit.

THE CONTRACTS

When you add financial planning to your practice, *full disclosure* is the operative phrase when dealing with your clients. Your broker/dealer will assist you in determining what type of contracts are required. Many of you already require a tax return engagement letter. I recommend getting these contracts and disclosure documents signed at the earliest opportunity. Clients should be allowed ample time to review the contracts alone and to have them explained to their satisfaction. However, we make it clear early that they must be signed in order for us to do business. Get them out of the way before you start completing applications for investments.

STAFF INVOLVEMENT

Staff Pre-Interview

Although many CPAs are reluctant to let their staff members have much contact with clients, other than to answer the phone or greet them when they come in, I believe that practice underutilizes a valuable resource and is poor time management. I have several staff members who are much better at some types of client contact than I am. If your staff members establish relationships with clients, they will feel more a part of the firm, turnover will be reduced, and clients will call them on minor matters instead of taking up your time.

I had some doubts as to whether my staff could handle any type of technical interview regarding tax returns or data gathering. Some personnel simply could not handle this type of interaction. For the most part, however, using staff to do some pre-interviews was successful.

We have our lowest-level staff pre-interview tax clients using a simple questionnaire. We decided to do this in order to send a direct message to our clients regarding the things they needed to do in order to let us serve them efficiently. When inadequacies in the data are caught at this level, senior-level staff time is saved. If the data is incomplete, the client can work with lower-level staff to get it complete before it goes to the preparer. This interview should be conducted in a client conference room or private office if at all possible.

We also let our senior staff interview clients and prepare tax returns. We prepared most returns with the clients present if they used organizers. Only a few clients objected to not seeing me as usual. I kept them on the same system as before. Eventually, 100 percent of our clients were converted. As long as you let them know that they have a choice, that you are not forcing them to do it your way, they will usually cooperate.

Staff Post-Interview

In those cases in which my senior staff developed excellent relationships with clients, they often requested to do the post-interview. As long as they were familiar with the correct forms and procedures, I allowed them to do so. This was especially helpful when my schedule was full and a client needed to pick up his or her return.

Filing Technical and Marketing Articles

Use staff to file. I endured much frustration in the early stages of business because I could never find that special article that I had read just two weeks earlier that would provide the solution for the problem I had today. I either couldn't remember where I had read it, or if I could, I couldn't remember what I had done with it.

The solution came when I set up two sets of ring binders for each item in my marketing plan. One set was for technical information, and the second set was for marketing and sales information. For example, I have one binder for 403(b) and 401(k) for technical articles and one for sales and marketing. The articles and technical memorandums are an excellent and quick referral source. I have used them repeatedly when clients brought in articles from a newspaper or magazine that caused them to worry about their investments. When I immediately produced two or three articles giving a more positive view, they felt more comfortable and were impressed that I was "on top of things."

5

Selling from the Financial Plan

Aside from the value of the post-tax interview, the discovery that financial plans were actually tools that could be used for selling, rather than regurgitations from boilerplate programs, was the most significant and profitable one I made in this profession.

Rather than being strictly academic in nature, financial plans actually add *sizzle* and *stick* to the sales process: sizzle because they tell a story that most clients have never heard before, and stick because clients are reluctant to leave the professional who has "their plan."

CPAs, in particular, should use financial plans for the following reasons:

1. *You need something tangible.* You are used to presenting your clients with a product. Even though the services you sell are intangible, almost all of your bills are for a tangible product of some kind. Tax returns, audit reports, financial statements—all are tangible. You deliver something tangible that your clients can see and touch when you send a bill. Without a written plan, you may have a hard time selling.

2. *Financial plans give you an education.* Only after I had completed my first plan for a client did I feel truly qualified to assist other clients in this profession. The creative process required in completing a plan will force you into creative thought about the particular client and the financial planning process itself.

3. *Financial plans give you something to talk about besides product.* When I used to try to sell from product illustrations, my tongue would get tied in knots and I would lose my train of thought. When the client throws you a curve, you can get back on track by referring to the plan.

4. *Plans provide good documentation for your files.* When a client calls for an appointment after a long absence to discuss his investments, you can review the plan to remember exactly why he is invested the way he is. You can't keep all of those things in your memory if you have more than 25 clients. A plan also provides a good defense if a competitor tries to take your client with the latest hot product.

5. *Plans distinguish you from the competition.* Few, if any, of your competitors ever prepare financial plans. If they do, they are generally "canned" plans.

6. *Plans help you to close the sale.* By the time you have gone through a creative process to arrive at a road map for your clients, you "own" the plan. When the client comes in to discuss it, you are convinced that it is the right thing to do. That conviction will come through in all aspects of the presentation, and your client will sense it.

7. *Plans enhance client retention.* Clients are extremely reluctant to leave the professional who designed their road maps to financial security.

8. *Plans attract continuous business.* Plans are both events and processes. They must be monitored and changed as circumstances change. A plan

becomes an evolving instrument. When circumstances or events demand changes, then you are the one with the plan. Changes often bring more sales.

9. *A plan creates a sense of obligation in the client's mind to at least listen to what you have to say.*

Given all these reasons, why don't most CPAs prepare plans? The following paragraphs may explain:

1. *The fee issue.* CPAs are used to getting paid directly for time expended on behalf of a client. Of course, most don't get paid for all this time, but we like to think that anyway. How do you charge for a financial plan when a learning curve is involved? Do you charge for the learning time? How much is it worth? "Better to not do one at all" becomes the excuse.

2. *The audit mentality.* We don't think we can do a plan unless the numbers are exactly right. "Well, Mr. Client, exactly what is the balance of your CD and how much of that is accrued interest?" *Forget audit.* You are dealing with projections that extend sometimes as far as 50 years. This is not an exact science, but an educated projection is better than no plan at all. If your client could provide you with exact figures for his financial statement, chances are he wouldn't need you at all.

3. *The projection freeze.* Most of our training is antiforecast. Forecasts have to be documented thoroughly. We have to place disclaimers on every page, and assumptions have to be clearly substantiated. Forecasts are dangerous.

Projections, however, are necessary in financial planning. These are not going to be reviewed by the general public, but are for your clients' use in planning their future.

4. *Lack of creative thinking.* "Where are the rules for filling in the forms? Where are the answers so I can see if I did this right?" Sorry, there are no correct answers. There are too many individual circumstances, personalities, and other factors involved to arrive at a perfect solution—which, among other things, makes this profession so exciting and rewarding. You can become a creative thinker with practice and the use of reminder checklists, which are discussed later.

If you are starting to agree that plans are good and that CPAs can prepare them, where should you start? *Do your own plan!*

GETTING THE BASICS

In order to prepare a plan, you must have certain information from the client. It must be reasonably accurate, although not necessarily perfect. How do you obtain it?

The ingredients essential to the smallest of plans are described in the following paragraphs:

1. *Goals.* You do not necessarily have to have all of the client's financial goals, but you must have at least the one or more that relate to the subject at hand. Discovering goals is the easiest and most rewarding part of the process. Most clients are both surprised and pleased when you ask what their goals are. Even if you are just asking for their goals in relation to one particular investment, they are still pleased.

If they don't know what their goals are, provide them with a goals sheet to spark their imagination. Ask them to rate their goals in order of importance.

2. *Risk tolerance.* Risk measurements are available from several sources, including product sponsors, the College for Financial Planning, the American College, and others. A short form, along with some probing questions, can determine the client's true risk tolerance. Statistics indicate that most people say that they will take more risk than they actually will. I have found that most of my clients will take more risks if they understand the nature of risk. Most do not understand purchasing-power risk or the risk-reward principle.

3. *Financial data (information for a personal financial statement).* Getting financial data sheets completed is often a stumbling block to the completion of a plan. I used to send forms home with a client to fill out. I never had a set returned. Now I assign the data-gathering process to staff who are tenacious in getting the necessary information without offending the client.

Most financial data sheets are either too lengthy and cumbersome or too short. We tried to design something in between that would provide most of the information we needed, yet still be easy to complete.

- Except in rare cases, don't rely on the client to complete the forms.
- The most efficient way to gather data is to do it when you can get the client's complete cooperation. That usually means doing it during tax season. If he is unable to provide the data at that time, send him a list of things to bring or send to you. Then keep following up until you get what you want.
- Don't forget that you have the most valuable piece of information about the client you can possibly have—his tax return. Use it to gather data. A major portion of the information you need can be determined from the return.

If you can gather these three basic items, you are ready to prepare a financial plan.

The actual preparation of financial plans is discussed in greater detail later, but it is wise to keep in mind the essential components, as presented to clients:

1. Goals.
2. Assets available to meet your goals (the financial statement).
3. Assets required to meet your goals.
4. Estate planning (when applicable).
5. How we recommend you reach your goals.

MAXI OR MINI-PLANS

Another common misconception of financial plans is that they are all "small books," too cumbersome to work with. Eighty percent of the plans we prepare are less than 12 pages in length. We keep to the basics, as described earlier. Length and complexity do not a good plan make. What does make a good plan is clarity, congruency with the client's goals and risk tolerance, and ease of implementation. If it doesn't have these qualities, you may have an academically correct, long, complex plan, but a poor plan.

How do you decide whether a client needs a full-blown plan or a modest one? The answers to the following questions can help:

1. How many opportunities does the client have? More problems usually mean a more extensive plan.
2. How much information will the client provide? If she won't sit still or provide you the information to do a complete plan, then do a mini-plan with a cover letter and agreement stating that she needs a bigger one, but has elected to go with a partial plan at this time.
3. Will the plan address a particular investment or problem? You can make a specialized plan that addresses only one investment the client owns or problem she has. This should lead to a more comprehensive plan later. Should you do a plan even when you are only considering changing a CD to a mutual fund? Yes. Review the advantages of doing a plan and the reasons. Even if your plan consists of only a cover sheet and a recommendation, do the plan!

PLANS PREPARED FROM THE TAX RETURN

Is it possible to prepare a plan from a tax return? I have argued more than once with programmers and other financial planners that it is possible. Such a plan may not be accurate to the last detail, but how many plans are? A financial statement that is accurate to the penny on a certain date will change before you can get it to the client.

Other than the client's goals, the most valuable source of information about the client can be taken from the tax return. The following list is a sample of what you can obtain from a return:

1. Personal data, such as addresses, children's names and ages, clients' names and ages.

2. Client's and spouse's salaries.

3. Interest income and approximate value of interest-bearing investments. If you have two years' tax returns and 1099s, a great deal of information on principal invested can be obtained. Just by division, using current and historical interest rates or yields, you can estimate the value of holdings that bear interest.

4. The value of stock or mutual funds (dividend yielding investments). Using dividend yields, you can estimate the value of stock.

5. Information about the client's business (if any): what kind it is, whether it has a retirement plan, and so forth.

6. Whether or not a client trades stocks (from Schedule D).

7. Whether or not the client has rental property, what she paid for it and when she bought it, how much income it brings in, and what is owed against it.

8. Whether the client has a farm, what she paid for it, when she bought it, what livestock and/or equipment is included.

9. Whether the client has an IRA or Keogh.

10. The amount of the mortgage on the client's personal residence (from Schedule A).

11. Most other debts the client has (from Schedule A).

These are just a few of the items that you can glean from current and prior tax returns. You can prepare a rough plan that will get your foot in the door for a more accurate plan if needed.

Should you do a rough plan from the tax return? If that will get the client's attention and cause her to take some needed course of action, you bet! Often, a rough plan drawn from the tax return will inspire the client to provide you with more complete information to do a comprehensive plan.

HOW PRODUCTS FIT INTO THE PLAN AND THE SALES PROCESS

In many prior instances in this book, I have mentioned that product is the least important part of the sales process. That doesn't mean that product

Form 5.2   Sample Investment Plan

PERSONAL INVESTMENT PLAN

Client _____

Date _____

Plan Implementation Steps
(Internal Use Only)

Client Authorization Date _____

Project	Due Date	Comp. ( )
_____	_____	_____
_____	_____	_____
_____	_____	_____
_____	_____	_____
_____	_____	_____
_____	_____	_____
_____	_____	_____
_____	_____	_____
_____	_____	_____
_____	_____	_____

is unimportant, just that a well-prepared plan is like a puzzle with a few missing pieces. When you know the shape of the pieces, it is easy to plug them into the puzzle. Products, of course, represent the missing pieces.

I almost never mention a specific product in the financial plans I prepare. Product recommendations are decided before I present the plan to the client, but I do not include them in the plan except in a generic fashion. Our standard financial plan format has an implementation sheet that lists all of the products to be used. The products are listed by amounts and, in accordance with goals, by number. We also try to list the source of funds for each product investment. The implementation sheet provides your staff and you with a nice paper trail to use when completing the transaction. It also is a good referral source when you are trying to trace the source of funds at a later date.

After the client has accepted the recommendations presented in the plan, we discuss products that will be used to implement it. My discussion is limited to the particular features and a reiteration of the risks involved.

These have usually been explained generically during conversation about the plan. After I have discussed the plan to the client's satisfaction, I turn the client over to my assistant who will go through the application, prospectus, and check-writing procedures. The client will again be reminded about risk and will have ample opportunity to ask any additional questions he or she may have.

What if a client insists on buying a product that you don't recommend? If it is a product that you simply cannot live with, then just refuse to implement the plan using this product. Better to lose the sale than to have an unhappy client tell others that you sold him something that didn't meet his needs. If the client insists on buying a product that we can live with but wouldn't recommend in this particular situation, we often go ahead with implementation as long as we get to implement the major portion of the plan using products that we do recommend and are comfortable with. In such instances, we ask the client to sign a disclaimer letter to avoid future misunderstandings. See Form 5.3.

Form 5.3   Sample Disclaimer Letter

_____   _____

_____   (Date)

_____

We recognize that our clients often desire to make investments that suit their particular personal needs. These investments may not coincide or may even conflict with basic financial planning concepts and principles. You have elected to make such an investment, and we have agreed to process the transaction for you and will be compensated for our services.

To avoid any future misunderstandings between ourselves or other interested parties, please sign below to indicate that you are making the following investment(s):

_____against our recommendations.

_____without any recommendation by any member of our firm.

Investment Description: _____

Amount: _____   Date: _____

_____   _____

Client Signature   Date

Don't try to sell based on yield or product. You are giving your client every reason to attack you with the same information later when conditions change. *Sell long-term solutions!*

Getting an Appointment After the Plan Is Prepared

We seldom fail to get a client to meet with us after a plan has been prepared. Our procedure, outlined in the following paragraphs, may produce the same results for you.

1. After the plan is prepared and ready for presentation, ask the receptionist or another assistant to call the client and announce that the plan is ready for his review. The caller will tell the client that you are going to mail it to him and would like to schedule an appointment to discuss it with him. *Never* try to set the appointment before the plan is actually ready for review! You can't take the risk of not giving the client time to review the plan before you go over it with him. You give him an automatic excuse to delay implementation if he hasn't had the plan for at least a couple of days before your appointment.

2. Allow the client about a week, no longer than two, for review time between the mailing date and the appointment date. If you allow a longer time, the plan gets cold. Do not mail the plan until an appointment has been set up. If you are doing the plan at no charge, you own it, not the client. If he won't give you a date for an appointment right away, tell him you will call back when he has a better idea of his schedule.

3. The day before the scheduled appointment, review the major points of the plan.

4. When the client comes in, ask him if he has had a chance to review the plan. You may get a strong clue if he brings in the plan in the same envelope you used for mailing with the seal unbroken. *That is not your problem.* If you try to present it to him on the same day of his appointment, then it *is* your problem. If the client has reviewed the plan extensively, start by asking him if he has any questions. If the client has not reviewed the plan, start by explaining it in a straightforward manner. In either case, continue as follows:

   a. Repeat the goals and make sure he understands that the goals are his, not yours (trust and opportunity questions here; see TOPS in Chapter 1).

   b. Repeat any problems he has in reaching his goals. You can take this information from the financial statement and the ''Assets Required'' section of the plan (mostly pain questions here).

   c. Go directly to your recommendations for meeting his goals. Turn with him to the Recommendations section and go over them item by item (solutions and comfort).

d. State that you have the paperwork ready to start him on the road toward reaching his goals.

e. Say no more.

f. Bring in the assistant to do the implementation.

g. After the checks are written and paperwork signed, you should step in to congratulate the client on his decision and ask whether he has any more questions on the products used. Make sure that he understands principal fluctuation, risks involved, and the long-term nature of the investment he is making. These will have been explained again by your assistant, using a form called a "Memorandum of Understanding." See Forms 5.4, 5.5, and 5.6.

To Charge or Not to Charge

We consider ourselves commission and fee-based planners, but 95 percent of our revenue comes from commissions. Our clients are quite fee resistant. This is because of the nature of the area we serve. There are no fee-based planners in our area. People are not used to paying fees for financial planning. They don't like to write checks to professionals unless they are paying for a necessary service. Others regions may be different. We do not charge fees for our plans. We like to think that we are sufficiently confident in our plans that our clients will implement them through us.

I usually set some standards for medium and large plans that take a considerable amount of time. I ask for assurance that if the client likes my suggestions, he or she will implement them through me. If the client implements the plan elsewhere, I will bill for time expended at my standard rate. In rare instances, I will agree to offset any fees with commissions earned. If commissions earned are sufficient to pay my fee, then there will be no fee charged. One other seldom-used procedure is to charge the client a minimum fee for the plan, regardless of whether it is implemented. I do this for clients with whom I have not had previous dealings and when the plan is fairly large. This gives me some protection for at least a recovery of direct costs. The key is *full disclosure*. Make sure the client understands the arrangement before you start.

Form 5.4 Sample Memorandum of Understanding (Mutual Fund and Other Investments)

MEMORANDUM OF UNDERSTANDING
MUTUAL FUND/OTHER INVESTMENTS

Client _____ Date _____
Investment Description _____

DO YOU UNDERSTAND?
  I. The principle of risk and the degree of risk involved with the investment I am making with your firm have been explained to me. My investment is primarily subject to the following types of risk:

Interest Rate	Market	Purchasing Power	Credit and Financial
_____	_____	_____	_____

                                                          _____
                                                          Initial

   I understand the risk/reward principle and have been shown the "Investment Pyramid."
                                                          _____
                                                          Initial
 II. I understand the difference between liquidity and marketability. My investment is considered to have _____ liquidity and _____ marketability.
                                                          _____
                                                          Initial
III. I understand that because of possible movements in markets or interest rates and the effect of commissions or surrender charges, I should consider this investment as long-term, allowing a period of at least _____ to _____ years for it to perform properly. This holding period is not mandatory, but highly recommended.
                                                          _____
                                                          Initial
IV. Commission and/or surrender charges applicable to this investment have been explained to me. My investment may be affected by a:
   _____Front Commission (%)   _____Back Commission
   _____Surrender Charge—Yr 1- %   Yr 3- %   Yr 5-   %
                            Yr 2- %   Yr 4- %   Yr 6-   %
   _____Other N/A

                                                          _____
                                                          Initial

By providing your signature below you are attesting that this sheet has been explained to you. You have been asked to sign it as indicated in the interest of full and complete disclosure. This is for your protection as well as ours.

Thank you for your cooperation!

_____   _____
Registered Representative   Client Signature
1st Global Capital Corp.

Form 5.5   Sample Memorandum of Understanding (Insurance Annuities)

MEMORANDUM OF UNDERSTANDING
INSURANCE ANNUITY PURCHASES

Client _____   Date _____

Investment Description _____

DO YOU UNDERSTAND?

I. The principle of risk and the degree of risk involved with the investment I am making with your firm has been explained to me. My investment is primarily subject to the following types of risk:

Interest Rate	Market	Purchasing Power	Credit and Financial
_____	_____	_____	_____

I understand the risk/reward principle and have been shown the "Investment Pyramid."   _____ Initial

II. I understand that while my investment is considered marketable because I can get my money out at any time by electing my choice of annuity options available, it is considered to have low liquidity. If I take my money out in a lump sum within the next _____ years, my earnings will be subject to the following surrender charges by the insurance company:

1st year	_____%	5th year	_____%
2nd year	_____%	6th year	_____%
3rd year	_____%	7th year	_____%
4th year	_____%	8th year	_____%

_____ Initial

III. I understand that the earnings rate of __% is guaranteed for the first _____ year(s), after which time the money will go in with other larger sums to earn at a rate that will fluctuate on a _____ basis.

_____ Initial

By providing your signature below you are attesting that this sheet has been explained to you. You have been asked to sign it as indicated in the interest of full and complete disclosure. This is for your protection as well as ours.

Thank you for your cooperation!

_____   _____
Registered Representative   Client Signature

_____   _____
Date   Date

Form 5.6   Sample Memorandum of Understanding
(403(b) Insurance Annuities)

MEMORANDUM OF UNDERSTANDING FOR 403(b)
INSURANCE ANNUITY PURCHASES

Client _____   Date _____
Investment Description _____

DO YOU UNDERSTAND?

I. The principle of risk and the degree of risk involved with the investment I am making with your firm has been explained to me. My investment is primarily subject to the following types of risk:

Interest Rate	Market	Purchasing Power	Credit and Financial
_____	_____	_____	_____

I understand the risk/reward principle and have been   _____
shown the "Investment Pyramid."   Initial

II. I understand that while my investment is considered market-able because I can get my money out at any time by electing my choice of annuity options available, it is considered to have low liquidity. If I take my money out in a lump sum within the next _____ years, my earnings will be subject to the following surrender charges by the insurance company.

1st year	_____%	5th year	_____%
2nd year	_____%	6th year	_____%
3rd year	_____%	7th year	_____%
4th year	_____%	8th year	_____%

_____
Initial

III. I understand that effective January 1, 1989, IRC Section 403(b) (11) prohibits the distribution of post-1988 salary reduction elective deferrals and earnings from my 403(b) contract, except in the event of one of the following:

(1) Attainment of age 59-1/2
(2) Separation from service
(3) Death
(4) Total and permanent disability
(5) Financial hardship (in which event only the contributions may be withdrawn)

_____
Initial

Form 5.6 (*Continued*)

IV. I understand that per Section 403(b) (11), if I take my money out prior to age 59-1/2, I will be subject to a 10% penalty by the IRS. I will also be taxed on the money as income in the year in which I take it out.

_____

Initial

V. I understand that the earnings rate of % is guaranteed for the first _____ year(s), after which time the money will go in with other larger sums to earn at a rate that will fluctuate on a _____ basis.

_____

Initial

By providing your signature below you are attesting that this sheet has been explained to you. You have been asked to sign it as indicated in the interest of full and complete disclosure. This is for your protection as well as ours.

Thank you for your cooperation!

_____	_____
Registered Representative	Client Signature
_____	_____
Date	Date

6

Selling with Mailers and Tangibles

I have said several times that you should not sell through using a product. Can you sell by mailing things to clients and potential clients? Can you do it by using product illustrations and hypotheticals?

Yes and no. Everything counts in the sum total of your ability to sell. It is impossible to measure the impact that mailers, illustrations, and hypotheticals have on sales. I consider them as a minor component in the entire sales process. They are tools that may complement the TOPS process for certain clients (see TOPS in Chapter 1).

A few cautions for CPAs:

1. Don't hide behind the tools you use. The only truly effective way to profitability in this business is to get face to face with clients. Most tools won't sell a thing for you.
2. Selling is a numbers game. The more presentations you make, the more sales you will make.
3. If you sell by product and performance, your relationships will be based on product and performance. We all know that products don't always perform as we hope they will.

PRODUCT SPONSOR MAILERS

The use of product sponsor mailers is a good idea. They are inexpensive and often free. Some sponsors will even help you with postage. Such mailers are professionally designed and may add to your own professionalism. They will position you with your clients as being in the investment business. Will they sell much directly? No. But if they get clients interested, then you can use TOPS questions and financial plans to cement the sale and the relationship.

PRODUCT SPONSOR WHOLESALERS AND STAFF

Engaging product sponsor wholesalers and staff is also worthwhile. They have a vested interest in your success. If you make money, they make money. They will assist you in client meetings, often pay for seminars, assist in advertising, give help on technical questions. These people constitute a valuable resource. Get a clear understanding of how the wholesaler makes money so that you can help her as she helps you.

Limit your products to only a few major sponsors. The more business you send to a product sponsor, the more she can afford to help you. Yet is this in the best interest of the client? Actually, I think it is. You can usually find a wide range of different types of products in only one or two mutual fund families. You have the ability to be thoroughly familiar with only a few products. The more you limit your offerings, the more familiar you will be. That seems to be in the client's best interest. If you develop a strong relationship with a product sponsor, you can get quick action on client requests or, in the event of errors, in their accounts.

HYPOTHETICALS AND ILLUSTRATIONS

I used to use hypotheticals a lot. These are past-performance illustrations that show what a particular hypothetical investment would have done over varying periods of time in the past. Software to do hypotheticals can be obtained from the particular mutual fund companies usually at minimum or no cost. It is also available from companies such as Morningstar and CDA. Using hypotheticals is a good way to learn about the historical performance of funds. You can transpose your client's current situation to the past and see what would have happened if he or she had made a particular investment over one, three, five, or ten years or other selected periods of time. Most software also allows you to use a combination of funds, different withdrawal strategies, and so forth. Hypotheticals provide comfort to you and your client about the historical performance of particular investment products. Be sure that appropriate warnings are given to your clients, that past performance is not a guarantor of future performance. Past performance is just one way of evaluating a product.

Don't base your selling to the client on a hypothetical illustration. Sell her on the idea of the product as the vehicle that allows her to solve her problem and to reach her long-term goals. Always emphasize the long-term nature of the investment.

Insurance illustrations are a different matter. They are not based on past performance but on current interest rates. I have found them to be a fairly ineffective sales tool because they are too confusing for the client to understand properly. Again, when selling insurance, you must use TOPS. You are selling solutions to problems, not illustrations.

Be cautious when using illustrations. I usually drop the interest rate a point below what is currently being paid so that my client can see the effect on his insurance if the yield drops. This is especially important in interest-sensitive products. You don't want your client to run out of insurance and cash value when your original illustration shows him with a sufficient death benefit and a hefty cash value.

We put a couple of cover sheets on our illustrations. One explains the terms used in the illustrations in simple language. The other is a ''Caution'' piece that basically says that I or anyone else can do almost anything with an insurance illustration by using different assumptions (see Form 6.1).

Form 6.1   Cover Letter—Caution

CAUTION

It is often said that an insurance professional had better be the "first and only" or the last person to prepare an insurance illustration. Unfortunately, this is true. If given the opportunity, we can also beat any competitive quote. This is true not only because we have a variety of insurance companies and products to choose from, but an infinite variety of "assumptions" that we can make regarding future interest rates, etc.

What does this mean to you, the consumer? It means that you must ask each professional you are dealing with what assumptions were made to arrive at the numbers in your illustration. The cheapest policy is not always the best policy! Be sure that your insurance professional has made realistic assumptions that are in your best interest. Always deal with professionals that you know and trust. We have prepared the attached illustrations using the best information available to meet your financial goals.

Thank you,

Registered Representative

USING YOUR OWN LETTERS

If you are going to communicate with your client through the mail, nothing is more effective than a personal letter. Even if you are mailing the same letter to a lot of clients, personalizing is effective. Here are some rules for effective communication:

1. *Keep it simple.* If a seventh-grader can't understand what you are saying, it's too complicated. CPAs have to be warned repeatedly about this. We have a need to be sure that the client knows how smart we are and often put that ahead of the need to communicate effectively.
2. *Keep it focused.* Don't try to cover every available topic in one letter. I have to watch myself constantly on this one. Don't let your reader wonder what the letter is really about after he or she has already read it.
3. *Talk about solutions or benefits.* Get to the point in plain English. Offer comfort and reassurance to the client who has problems.

4. *Read the letter as if you were the client.* How do you feel when you get home from a hard day's work and find a three-page, difficult-to-read letter? What is your reaction?

5. Write the way you talk—that is, assuming that you use good grammar. Don't break the basic rules.

6. *Keep the trust.* Remember that clients buy from you because they trust you. Make your letter as personal and friendly as possible. Remind them of how much you know about them.

7. *Make it as short as possible.* Most people are short on time.

8. *Be sure your letter matches your reader.* Don't write something that is appropriate for one client but inappropriate for the one whom you are addressing.

9. *Don't assume what your client knows, feels, or likes.* The client may not know what you are talking about, and may not share your love for the Dallas Cowboys.

Form 6.2   Penny Pincher Cover Letter

THE PENNY PINCHER

Many of you have heard people described by the old adage as "penny wise and pound foolish." That truly describes the money habits of many people. However, most people who are penny wise are also pound wise. They know how to turn their pennies into dollars. In the following pages we will try to tell you how to be penny wise and dollar wise. We will tell you:

How to Keep Your Money
(Keep it from slipping through your fingers)

How to Save Your Money

Where to Put Your Money

We hope you can use these helpful hints in your savings and investment program. These are only broad-based hints to be used as reminders and as part of our overall financial planning program. Please contact us about our other services.

Sincerely,

Registered Representative

Form 6.3 Penny Pincher #1.

PENNY PINCHER #1

How to Keep Your Money
(Keep it from slipping through your fingers)

1. Don't Be a Big Spender
Stop having guilt feelings because you don't spend enough. Overspending is often related to insecurity. However, some of our social standards have made it the other way around. Savers and wise spenders are usually more secure than those who overspend regularly. You have nothing to prove by overspending.

2. Keep Minimal Cash
Stop carrying so much cash in your pocket. Money in your jeans makes you feel "flush." It's just too darned easy to spend. Make spending money a little more troublesome by carrying less in your pockets.

3. Wants vs. Needs
Establish your priorities. Is something you want just a "whim" or is it a really valid want? What is it really worth to you? Ask yourself these questions every time you buy a "want purchase" rather than a "need purchase." Learn how to distinguish wants from needs. If you sincerely desire or want some products or services that you do not necessarily need, make a list of those items and put it aside. Sometimes a want will disappear entirely or at least will not become quite so nagging. This will save you from lots of impulse purchases, but won't deny you all of your wants. Use your want list as a motivation to save for what you want, rather than using credit to buy it.

4. Cheap Saturday Nights
If you think that a good way to spend a cheap Saturday night is to visit your local discount store and shop—forget it. That can be one of the most expensive forms of entertainment, because you'll buy things that you don't need. If you don't buy them on the spot, you'll make a mental note to go back and get them later. Most of the things you buy, you probably could have done without.

5. Stop Chasing Sales
Don't be a sale chaser. Don't go all over town searching for the cheapest item or chasing items that are advertised as being on sale. Watch only for sale items that you truly need and would have pur-

(Continued)

Form 6.3   (*Continued*)

chased anyway. Also, remember the cost of traveling from one place to another or to an out-of-the-way location. I've seen people travel 40 miles to save two dollars. With the cost of gasoline and automobiles today, that is truly "penny wise and pound foolish."

6. Don't Buy on Impulse

Don't use impulse purchases to scare away the doldrums. Instead, reward yourself occasionally with one of the items on your want list after you have saved adequately for it. That way, your thriftiness is rewarded and you will feel better after the purchase. Did you ever notice what some people refer to as the "post-purchase blues" or "buyer's remorse"? You usually suffer these feelings after you have made an impulsive purchase for something that you did not necessarily need. If you find yourself suffering like this often, then you are doing too much impulse buying.

7. Avoid Credit Card Whiplash

Don't get caught in a credit card "whiplash." That's caused by whipping out your credit card every time you want something, rather than waiting until you can afford to pay for it. Try to avoid using your credit card totally on "snowball purchases." These are purchases that tend to melt away or are used up in a relatively short period of time. A good example is a vacation. Save for your vacations ahead of time. Everyone deserves vacations, but they're often ruined when you are left with a credit card bill when you get back. I do not advocate tearing up your credit cards unless you are a chronic overbuyer, but I do advocate using credit wisely.

8. Use Credit Wisely

On the subject of credit, some people believe that you should pay cash for everything. That's not necessarily a bad habit, but it often leads to bad financial management. Sometimes, I recommend borrowing for two reasons: (1) Borrowing gives you leverage (allows you to use other people's money instead of your own). It works when you wisely invest your own funds. (2) Borrowing can often be self-inflicted discipline for *saving*. Sound strange? I have found that my clients will generally pay the bank or other creditors. If they don't, the consequences of not paying will be made very evident to them by their creditors. However, if you don't pay yourself back for savings that you've dipped into, there will be no one to cry foul.

9. Be Your Own Banker

Pay your own insurance and taxes on your personal residence or other real estate. Don't let your mortgage company hold your funds

Form 6.3 *(Continued)*

---

in escrow without paying you interest. Establish your own interest-bearing escrow account that you use to pay insurance and taxes. Caution: Be sure that you fund your own escrow account and that you have money available to pay your insurance and taxes when they come due.

10. Keep It in the Family
Make budgeting, saving, and financial management a family matter. Discuss it with your spouse and children. If everyone doesn't know what the common goals are, everyone suffers.

Form 6.4   Penny Pincher #2

PENNY PINCHER #2

HOW TO SAVE YOUR MONEY

1. Pay Yourself First
I know that is a tired old saying, but it works. Every time you receive your pay, put part of it back for yourself in a savings account or other savings instrument. If you put it in your checking account or in your pocket, you can "color it gone."

2. Let It Ride
If you have money in a money market, CD, or mutual fund, let your interest accumulate. Don't withdraw it unless you need it for an emergency or you are retired and are using it for living expenses. Let it accumulate. You will be amazed at how large sums of money can be accumulated on small investments.

3. Separate Your Savings
Separate your savings, either mentally or physically, for specific wants and needs. For example, you may have one money market fund for vacation and another for college education. Don't be upset if you don't have enough funds to practice this type of segregation. You can do it by using a simple notepad to segregate one account. If you don't have enough money now to have a minimum balance for a bank money market account, see us about a "no minimum" money market fund. You do need to separate, either mentally or physically, the funds that you have available for discretionary spending and those that you consider long-term growth funds.

(Continued)

Form 6.4   (*Continued*)

4. Consider Yourself to Have Two Jobs
It is a good idea to think of yourself as having two jobs. One is for your employer, which pays for living expenses. The other is for yourself. That makes it a little simpler to put back a small amount of your paycheck each month. Some people look upon saving as punishment and, therefore, very difficult to do. Remember that the funds are still yours and still available for expenditure; you have just separated them to make future purchases or for other specific reasons.

5. You Should Establish Goals
Don't be ultrasophisticated when you establish goals. It's OK to say that you want to save for your children's education or to provide funds for retirement. Be more specific and separate your long-term goals into shorter ones. For example, you may want to save $5,000 for a down payment on a new car. You may want to save up to six months of your salary as an emergency fund. Most financial advisors agree that you should have at least six month's salary as an emergency fund. I call that "sleep money." Read, update, and reread these goals often.

Form 6.5   Penny Pincher #3

PENNY PINCHER #3

WHERE TO PUT YOUR MONEY

Where to put your money is a broad subject that cannot be covered in a simple one-page letter, but the short listing here covers the more common generalized types of investments and savings accounts available to you.

1. Checking Accounts That Pay Interest
Ask your banker about NOW accounts and Super NOW accounts. The banking market is much more competitive and open than it was just a few years ago. Many banks offer varying competitive rates of interest on different types of checking accounts. Be sure you understand the interest rates that are being paid and the restrictions regarding minimum balances and so forth on the account before you take the plunge.

Form 6.5 *(Continued)*

2. Passbook Savings Accounts
In most cases, passbook savings accounts are poor investments, but they often provide a good method of saving small amounts of money until you can move them into accounts with more competitive rates. Most passbook accounts pay the lowest rates available anywhere, and several banks now have minimum balance requirements.

3. Money Market Accounts
Money market accounts are usually separated into mutual funds and accounts offered by banks. Mutual funds can best be described as a group of investors with "mutual interest" who pool their money and hire a manager to invest it for them in the money market. This manager will usually buy larger certificates of deposit and other money market instruments than you could afford to buy yourself. I consider them to be an excellent, safe method of investing at a fairly good interest rate. This is a good place to keep your money while you are waiting to invest in more aggressive or growth-oriented types of instruments.

4. Certificates of Deposit
CDs are available from banks, savings and loans, and some brokers. You usually have to invest your money for a specified period of time at a fixed rate.

5. Savings Bonds
Investment in savings bonds has long been overlooked by savers, but is now very much back in favor because of the competitive interest rate and the tax deferral feature. Don't disregard these as part of your savings program.

6. Stock Market or Equity Type Investments
Historical evidence says emphatically that most of us cannot be successful at picking stocks and actively trading in the market. The same body of evidence also says that you must own stocks to enjoy growth in your investment portfolio and protect yourself from inflation. So how do you own stocks without picking them. Mutual funds are professionally managed and offer even small investors the opportunity to enter the market and achieve diversification. Growth in the value of stocks is not taxed until the stocks are sold.

7. Tax-Favored Investments

• Real estate
  Real estate is favored with many provisions of the Internal Revenue Code, including depreciation. Be sure that you understand

(Continued)

Form 6.5 *(Continued)*

these and the property you are investing in, or the partnership you are buying a part of, before you take the plunge. Real estate investment trusts provide the small investor with a means to invest in real estate and still have liquidity.

- Equity investment or stock market
  See item 6.

- Individual retirement accounts
  If you don't have an individaul retirement account, get one. I consider these to be one of the best tax shelters available now. There are a myriad of ways that you can invest in individual retirement accounts, and you may need to seek counseling.

8. Tax-Exempt Investments
Tax-exempt investments usually pay a lower rate because they are not taxable. Learn now to calculate your effective after-tax yield on investments like these before you invest. Ask your financial planner how this works and how it relates to your tax bracket.

9. Shifting Income to Other Family Members
A good tax tactic is to move earnings on invested funds from your large tax bracket to your child's small or nonexistent tax bracket. It can be an excellent way to fund a child's education. Seek guidance.

10. Annuities
Annuities are another good means of building a retirement fund while deferring taxes on some of the earnings or contributions. Again, seek counseling before you invest.

11. Your Personal Residence
The home you live in is a shelter in more ways than one. Be sure you understand the tax implications of buying and selling a personal residence. Call us before you make major decisions on house purchases.

These are just a few general descriptions of the methods available to you to build a nest egg for retirement. We can explain or expand on any of these suggestions at your request. Call us.

Finally, don't get so caught up in pinching pennies that you don't enjoy your money. You can enjoy it better with a plan.

10. *Don't use business buzzwords.* Leave out the acronyms and terms peculiar to the industry. Your client will appreciate it.

11. *Watch the details.* Spell the names correctly, get the address right, don't misspell words.

We often give copies of our ''Penny Pinchers'' to clients, along with a cover letter (see Form 6.2), as shown in Forms 6.3, 6.4, and 6.5. Feel free to duplicate these pages for your clients. The message is basic and has special appeal for parents with children in their twenties.

7

Marketing to Small Businesses

If your firm is similar to mine, approximately 25 percent of your clients are small businesses. They represent a way to grow your own business exponentially. This chapter discusses some of the opportunities available and gives some hints on how to take advantage of them.

PAYROLL DEDUCTION PLANS

A payroll deduction plan represents a great opportunity that is under-utilized and undermarketed. The program can be carried out without IRS approval, costs the employee nothing, and is a great fringe benefit. It simply offers employees a way to save through payroll deduction. Numerous surveys have shown that employees had rather save through payroll deduction over any other method of saving. Even though it costs the employer almost no trouble and no expense, the plan is perceived by employees as a benefit. Several product sponsors offer a program that allows the employer to simply withhold funds from the employees' paychecks and submit one check to the product sponsor.

RETIREMENT PLANS AND CAFETERIA PLANS

Many of us are reluctant to sell retirement plans because of administration complexity and a perceived resistance by employers to any kind of contribution on behalf of employees. However, through our tax knowledge, CPAs can show employers how it can be very cost-effective to establish a retirement plan for employees in order for the employer to save on his or her own taxes. A good retirement plan will also reduce turnover and make recruiting new employees easier.

The administrative complexity and plan selection problems can be solved in a variety of ways. Third-party administrators are available to handle administration. Moreover, these administrators or product sponsors will prepare proposals for your client, complete with recommendations as to the type of plan to be implemented.

The possibilities for income for the registered representative in retirement planning are enormous. For example, a 25-employee business with average contributions of 6 percent on average salaries of only $30,000 would yield annual commissions of approximately $1,800. If you set up only four small plans like this for 10 years, your annual revenues would be approximately $80,000. This would be almost "automatic" revenue.

You can imagine the possibilities that are opened in new relationships with companies of 1,000 employees including approximately 100 executives.

So how do you sell retirement plans? Use TOPS (as described in Chapter 1).

Trust

Ask only one or more trust questions, such as, "Joe, your business is continuing to show good profits, and Uncle Sam seems to keep right on taking a larger and larger share. How long have you and I talked about doing something about it? Tax laws limit our choices, but sheltering income and putting off the taxes on the income it earns is still available to businesses like yours."

Opportunity

(If he already has a plan) "Do you completely understand the costs and benefits of the plan you currently have? What information were you provided to help you in your choice? Do your employees understand the plan and its benefits? Do they perceive it as a benefit that would be difficult to leave? What kind of participation do you get?"

(If no plan) "Is turnover costing you money? Do you know about what it costs to train a new employee and to absorb new employee errors? How are you going to make this business provide you with a comfortable retirement without taxes cutting too big a slice?"

Pain

"How many years have you owned this business? Do you have other sources of retirement? How do you feel about getting hit for Social Security taxes last year of about $_____ as well as unemployment taxes of about $_____? And that is just on your employees. What about the taxes you paid on your own earnings? How important is it to you to assist your employees in reaching a comfortable retirement? How important is it to you to make this business provide *you* with a comfortable retirement? Under present conditions, how is it going to do that?"

Solution

"What does retirement mean to you in terms of income, activities, and so forth? What do you want to do, and how much do you think it will take to do it?"

"If you could find a way to sock away some of your hard-earned dollars and keep the IRS away from it, how important would that be to you?"

Listen.

"What if I could also show you how to lower your Social Security taxes on employees' wages (cafeteria plan) and provide them an income tax break as well?"

Listen.

"Which is more important, providing for your own retirement or providing employee benefits and reducing turnover and costs?"

Listen.

"Would you be interested in a plan that allows you to receive the lion's share of the contributions?" (age weighted plan, nonqualified plan).

Listen.

"If you don't want to contribute anything for the employees, would it be important to you to set up a plan that provides only for you?" (charitable trust, nonqualified plan).

Listen.

"What about a plan that uses only employee money?" (401(k)).

Listen.

"If I could show you a way to contribute to the plan and use it as a way to provide for employees' retirement plans and take a tax deduction, while incurring only administrative expense, would that be of interest to you?" (401(k) with ER contribution substituted for raises in one period. This is a good deal for employees who do not have to pay income taxes on the raise, and the employer gets a deduction without substantial out-of-pocket costs.)

Of course, you generally would not have to ask all of these questions of every employer; usually one of them will be the hot button you are looking for.

BUY-SELL AGREEMENTS

A buy-sell agreement sounds like something that an attorney sells, doesn't it? If your small business prospect has two or more owners, chances are it needs a buy-sell agreement that provides for either disability or death of any of the primary owners. So how do you make money on this? You sell the disability and life policies on each owner.

Who writes the agreement? Either the client's attorney or one with whom you work. Most insurance companies will provide prototype plans to be reviewed by attorneys.

How do you sell? Use TOPS.

Trust

Begin with a trust question such as this:

"How long have you two been partners? I see from your tax return that the ownership is 50-50. Any of your family members involved in the business at this time?"

Listen.

Opportunity

Next, ask opportunity questions:
   "Does anybody know how to do the part of the business that Joe does?"

Listen.

"How about Tom?"

Listen.

"Do you have any kind of agreement that specifies what happens if one of you is disabled or dies?"

Listen.

Pain

Continue the conversation with pain questions:
   "Joe, would you be comfortable being partners with Tom's wife?"

Listen.

"Does she know as much as Tom does about running the business?"

Listen.

"Tom, since Joe is not married and his only heir is his 13-year-old son, how are you going to deal with being partners with Joe, Jr.?"

Listen.

"Since he is under age, who will be his guardian?"

Listen.

"None named?"

Listen.

"Then your partner will be a judge and a lawyer?"

Listen.

"Do you have time to report monthly to the court on operations of the business?"

Listen.

"You'll buy them out, you say?"

Listen.

"Without strapping the business for cash?"

Listen.

"What about the tax consequences of drawing that much money?"

Listen.

Aren't these easy pain questions?

Solution

Finally, ask solution questions, such as the following:
"How important is it to you to be able to draw money from the business if you are disabled?"

Listen.

"Do you want your wife to get a fair price for her share of the business?"

Listen.

"Is it important that the business continue?"

Listen.

"If I can show you how to avoid all these problems with a relatively pain-less plan today, are you prepared to do it?"

This is one of the easiest sales to be made, because the pain questions are so practical and real. Yet, most financial professionals don't make the sale because they get hung up on the issues of cross-purchase or entity (stock redemption) agreements. I have found that circumstances usually dictate which method is more appropriate. You have to consider who has the funds to pay the premiums, how many owners there are, and the possibility of alternative minimum tax, but these can be handled easily with assistance from the attorney, your broker-dealer's technical support, or the insurance company.

KEY EMPLOYEE BENEFITS

If your client wants to provide benefits for key employees without provid-ing for all employees or expensive reporting to the IRS, you can assist him or her with a nonqualified plan providing excellent retirement benefits for key employees.

BUSINESS SUCCESSION

Most small business owners do not have a plan to take the benefits of a lifetime of work out of their companies. They may want to pass on the business to children, sell it to employees, or sell it to an outside buyer.

They may not realize that estate and/or income taxes may prevent their dreams from being realized. Estate taxes may require the forced sale of the business in event of death. Income taxes may prevent the owner from receiving the income he expects from the sales proceeds. It is often a shock to see taxes take from 30 to 50 percent of a business's proceeds. This opens opportunities for charitable remainder trusts, ESOPS, life insurance to provide estate liquidity, key employee insurance, and disability insurance.

Most clients respond to these typical TOPS pain questions: "Did you know that the IRS is going to take up to 55 percent of your estate that exceeds $600,000 when you die? That they will get more than any heir you have designated? If the tax amounts to ($550,000), will your business be able to take that kind of cash hit? Could your children or wife sell it quickly? Would it bring full value if it had to be sold within nine months of your death? (There are certain relief provisions for family-owned businesses, but I've never had a client who made these provisions.)

GROUP LIFE, HEALTH, AND DISABILITY INSURANCE

Ask, "Does having a large group of employees buying these commissionable products automatically every month by payroll deduction appeal to you?"

FINANCIAL PLANNING AS A COMPANY BENEFIT

For medium-size or large companies, offering financial planning is a great way to provide a low-cost benefit to the employees that they will be grateful for. If you do the planning workshops right, the employees will receive a value that will be a permanent part of their lives. You can either charge a fee for the workshops (paid by the employer or shared by employees and employer) or elect to do the workshops for free just to get prospects for your services or products.

8

Success with Seminars

Are seminars an effective method of prospecting and familiarizing clients with your new services? Yes. Other than the post-tax interview, seminars were the most effective way to position ourselves as more than just tax accountants. They are especially effective for CPAs, because there is a client base to draw from. If a CPA gives a seminar, some of his or her clients almost always show up.

Are seminars cost-effective? They are—99 percent of our seminars have paid for themselves within the first month after presentation. There is no way to measure the payoff in the future, but I am convinced they continue to pay for years. I have had many seminar participants visit me for the first time years after the seminar was held. Moreover, seminars can be held at little or no cost. Product sponsors will often assist you. It is not necessary to go to great expense, because you already have an audience in your client base. Most of the huge expenses associated with seminars are for advertising and mailings to large numbers of people in order to get a few participants. You don't have to buy a mailing list. Just start with your own clients if you want to keep costs down.

OVERCOMING FEAR OF PUBLIC SPEAKING

Most people fear public speaking more than they do death. If you are one of these people, try some of the following suggestions.

- *Pick a friendly audience for your first try.* People who know you will forgive you if you are a little nervous. If you are a member of a service club, ask to speak on a subject that you are comfortable about. A natural, of course, is taxes.
- *Study the subject of public speaking.* There are many books on public speaking. Try these: *I Can See You Naked* by Ron Hoff, *How to Write and Give a Good Speech* by Joan Detz, *The Eloquent Executive* by William Parkhurst, and *How to Be a Good Speaker*, Research Institute of America, Inc.
- *Join Toastmasters or a similar teaching organization.* The benefits of joining such a group will reach into many areas of your life. Your confidence will increase, interpersonal skills will improve, and you will learn to stand in front of an audience without being so self-conscious that you feel naked.

USING SEMINARS TO ATTRACT BUSINESS

Can you use seminars as a way to attract business? Yes. However, I believe that your success will be limited unless you are the focal point of the seminar. You must come across as the person in charge. If you get others to give the seminar, be sure that they position you and your staff as the experts on the subject.

Where do you get speakers? Here are a few sources:

1. *Product sponsors.* Most wholesalers have to be pretty good presenters in order to survive. They will be happy to assist you with presenting. However, I prefer that they talk generically and not too much about their products. If they are going to assist you, it is only fair that some credit be given to their companies and products. They will often help you with the cost of the seminar.

    If you have clients in attendance who are considering investing in or have already invested in the products being mentioned, having a third party reaffirm their choice can be very effective. Just don't use a hard sale during the seminar.

2. *Your staff.* Even if you are uncomfortable in speaking at a seminar, maybe your staff isn't. If so, let them show their stuff. Maybe it will motivate you to speak at the next event.

3. *Authors and other professionals.* Often, a person wants to plug a book that has a relationship to a seminar that you are giving. For example, if we are planning a seminar on responsible investing, we invite the author of a book on the subject to speak on the environmental and social issues. We also have had psychologists speak on adjusting to life after work at seminars on retirement planning.

Tips on Presentation to a Group

1. Tell them what you are going to tell them, then tell them, then tell them what you told them. This is a good outline for any speech. Many people have short attention spans and low retention levels, making it necessary to say the same things in detail and summary format.

2. Use a conversational tone. Talk *to* your audience, rather than *at* them. Unless you are a practiced orator, it is best not to try to "preach" to an audience. Talk to them as you would in a normal conversation.

3. Involve your audience. Remember this rule: "Tell me and I will forget, show me and I will remember, involve me and I will understand." Ask questions. Use members of the audience as illustrations. Tell stories of personal experiences involving your subject matter.

4. Read from text sparingly. If you are going to read, you may as well hand out your prepared speech and leave the room.

5. Use various voice inflections, facial expressions, and your hands and body to illustrate points. It is good to show some emotion if you feel strongly about your subject, but this is not the time for faking it.

6. Get out from behind the lectern occasionally.

7. Forgive yourself. If you lose your place or don't know the answer to a question, just admit it. The audience will forgive you.

8. Keep it short and simple. Only the most gifted orator can keep an audience's attention for more than half an hour. In a seminar, you can go for an hour and a half if you are able to provide relief breaks for your audience and if you can break your presentation into digestible parts.

> "Most great leaders I've met are simple men. People like Sam Walton and General Schwarzkopf—they're far from stupid, but they are basically very simple. I hate complexity. The world is already complex enough without me making it more so. The principles of management and leadership are simple. The hard part is doing them, living up to them day after day, not making lots of excuses for ourselves."
>
> —H. Ross Perot

9. Use visual aids. Be sure they can be read from anywhere in the room. We like to use overheads. They are easy to make, and the equipment is inexpensive. Most people are primarily visual learners. Be sure to keep your visual aids simple and understandable. Don't try to impress people with your ability to put together rows of numbers. You'll just put them to sleep.

10. Handouts—use them, don't abuse them. When I go to a seminar, I hate to have the presenter show some wonderful overheads or wave a great information packet before my eyes, then fail to hand it out. "I wish I had some of these to give to you people" is a sure sign of a poorly prepared or thoughtless speaker. If you're going to show something, be prepared to give it to your audience.

When should you deliver handouts? That depends on your type of presentation. If you are using overheads that require analysis or worksheets that need filling in, have someone hand them out just before you use them. However, be cautious about giving handouts that will steal your show. If you give them out in advance, your audience may read them rather than listen to you. They will almost certainly get ahead of you or stay behind you unless you exercise a great deal of control and relate your presentation to your material very effectively.

If you are going to hand out materials and refer to them, number the pages! How many times have you been in a seminar and had a speaker say that he was working off the 42nd page of section 7 when there were no tabs to identify sections and no page numbers?

SEMINAR CHECKLIST

Because I dislike reinventing the wheel and trying to remember what mistakes we made last time, I recommend making a seminar checklist. Break it up into preliminary preparation, site preparation, on-site duties, presentation, and follow-up. See Form 8.1.

Form 8.1 Sample Seminar Checklist

SEMINAR CHECKLIST

Preliminary Preparation	Resp.	Due Date	Complete
1. Identify target audience.			
2. Select sites and times.			
3. Prepare client and non-client lists.			
4. Prepare mailings and invitations.			
5. Complete mailing two weeks prior for receipt on Monday or Tuesday.			
6. Prepare advertising copy.			
7. Arrange for ads to run in appropriate media (be sure to specify ad size and location).			
8. Prepare and mail news releases if seminar is designed for general public education.			
9. Notify local Chamber of Commerce and give handouts.			
10. Follow up if response to mail and ads isn't adequate. Follow up with phone calls beginning three days prior to date of seminar.			
11. Confirm reservations on day prior to and day of seminar.			
12. Select handouts and group in order.			
13. Prepare rough outline of seminar topic.			

Form 8.1 (*Continued*)

Site Preparation

1. Room temperature set 5 degrees below normal. _____ _____ _____

2. Shades drawn and distractions removed or hidden from view. _____ _____ _____

3. Lighting and glare checked. _____ _____ _____

4. Seating (short); space (adequate); chairs arranged for best view of presenter and visual aids (have extra chairs hidden but ready for use). _____ _____ _____

5. Visual aids in working order:
   a. Grease board or flip chart, markers, erasers _____ _____ _____
   b. Overhead projector and screen _____ _____ _____
   c. Slides and projector _____ _____ _____
   d. Lighting monitor assigned _____ _____ _____
   e. Other materials needed _____ _____ _____

6. Handouts readily available but under our control. _____ _____ _____

7. Evaluation and appointment sheet ready. _____ _____ _____

8. Business cards on hand for presenter. _____ _____ _____

9. Name tags for staff and participants (staff tags should have firm name). _____ _____ _____

10. Refreshments arranged. _____ _____ _____

(*Continued*)

Form 8.1 *(Continued)*

On-Site Duties	Responsibility
1. Greeting participants.	_____
2. Registering participants. (Write names. If person is not an existing client, include address and phone number.)	_____
3. Issuing name tags.	_____
4. Refreshments.	_____
5. Break and group "control."	_____
6. Facility "tour" director.	_____
7. Handouts (including business cards). Be sure all handouts are properly stamped.	_____
8. Evaluation sheets and setting appointments (extremely important!).	_____
9. Calendars for setting appointments.	_____

Note: In scheduling appointments with seminar attendees, schedule their beginning appointment time 15 minutes in advance so that staff can interview and gather as much information as possible regarding where their investments are (use form). Have office management set up files.

Presentation Reminder List

	Responsibility
1. Introduce yourself or have staff member introduce you.	_____
2. Introduce other staff members, always referred to as *associates*, not employees. Staff shouldn't group together. For those who are to assist with handouts, aisle seats are a good choice.	_____
3. State the purpose of the seminar:	_____
a. Goals for participants	_____
b. Goals for us—state why we're doing it; why we're qualified; what we're trying to specialize in.	_____
4. Have two staff members hand out your business cards.	_____
5. Announce break times, restroom locations, etc.	_____
6. Announce that handouts will be available.	_____

Form 8.1   (*Continued*)

---

7. Follow seminar outline. _____

8. Use only "audience participation"-type
handouts during seminar. _____

9. Summarize your presentation (reinforce the
need for audience to act on our suggestions). _____

10. Ask for questions. _____

11. Have at least two staff members distribute
handouts (describe each handout prior to
physically passing it out). Distributions
should be quick to keep the flow going. _____

12. As handouts are distributed, repeat our qualifications, goals, and no-cost services. _____

13. Hand out evaluation sheets and appointment
cards. Ask participants to complete them
now! Have pads or clipboards available for
writing on. _____

14. Staff should collect all evaluations, introduce
themselves, and set up appointments on calendar, if possible. _____

15. Thank-you and close. _____

SEMINAR FOLLOW-UP

	Resp.	Due Date	Complete
1. Review evaluation sheets—next day.	_____	_____	_____
2. Call to schedule appointments for people who responded positively—*next day.*	_____	_____	_____
3. Send "thank-you for attending" notes with additional marketing data within three days (send goals sheet).	_____	_____	_____
4. Call to confirm day prior to appointment. Remind the potential client to bring tax returns, IRA, CD, and other investment statements.	_____	_____	_____

(*Continued*)

8.1 *(Continued)*

5. Add names to potential
   client list. (Q & A).   _____   _____   _____

6. Financial planner must
   then follow through with
   a plan or suggestions for
   the client. If we do not,
   why even have a semi-
   nar?   _____   _____   _____

Note: Follow-ups are as important as the seminar itself. Your best and most experienced staff should be used. Assume clients are interested and want to talk to you, and let them know you sincerely think you can help them to achieve their goals, as stated in the seminar.

Preliminary Preparation

After stagefright, the second most common reason for not holding seminars is the fear that nobody will come. The preliminary preparation is to ensure that does not happen. Could it happen anyway? Yes, but it's highly unlikely. Of approximately 75 seminars we have held, we had to cancel only one for lack of interest. When we reviewed our list, we had not done all of the preliminary steps. We have had sparse attendance several times, however. What to do in this case? Go ahead as if you had a packed house. Try to give everyone special attention and make it a workshop environment rather than just a group presentation.

Site Preparation

In the next section of your checklist, be sure to include items that are necessary in preparing the site of the seminar. Typical concerns are room temperature, lighting, readiness of visual aids and handouts, and arrangements for refreshments.

On-Site Duties

An important part of the checklist is to ensure that no on-site details are overlooked in greeting the participants, getting name tags, evaluation sheets, and other needed materials.

Presentation Reminder List

Review the presentation section of the checklist just before you present so that you don't forget important things, such as introducing yourself, your staff, and special guests. Exercise caution with handouts, as described earlier.

Follow-Up

If you are not going to follow up, then why give the seminar? It is absolutely essential. Yet this is where most fail. Follow-up is more uncomfortable than speaking. We may be rejected. Make sure, however, to include follow-up in your planning and on your checklist.

9

Other Marketing Tips

Most of this book is directed to CPAs who already have clients. What if you do not? You can use the same techniques for gathering clients with slight modification. Use the rules of good time management, use seminars and the other tools described, keep prospecting all the time, set goals, and position yourself differently from the competition.

I have been amazed that most CPAs want to go after the "big elephants." They also chase the most esoteric products and schemes. I don't know what drives this tendency unless it is the basic human desire to get rich quick with minimal effort. It is especially ironic because most of our practices were built "one tax return at time." If your client base is small and wealthy, then elephant hunting may be for you. If not, then go after the sitting ducks. The elephants will present themselves between ducks.

All through this book, the importance of building relationships is stressed. If you want long-term success in this business, you will be relationship oriented rather than transaction oriented. That means you will maintain contact with the client after the sale.

1. Return your phone calls promptly.
2. Report to your clients regularly on the status of their investments.
3. Consider it a race to call your clients first before they call you in the event of a negative occurrence.
4. Send thank-you notes or letters after transactions are completed.

MORE CLIENT SERVICE IDEAS

As a CPA, you have spent many years building relationships with your clients. You should use that same commitment to service in providing financial planning and investment services to your clients. Don't be fooled into thinking that *performance* of investments is the key to client retention. *Communication* is the key to keeping clients, generating new business from existing clients, and getting referrals for new ones.

Communicate, communicate, communicate. *People don't care how much you know until they know how much you care.* Let your clients know that you care by keeping in contact on a regular basis.

Send status and performance reports. In good or bad times, you must send your clients reports on the status of their investments. It does not matter that they are getting reports from a mutual fund or insurance company; they bought the investment from *you*. You are the person they want to hear from. This is doubly important when performance has been poor. Write your clients a personal note on their reports to let them know you are watching the investment and remember the goals set by you and your client. Supplement this with a phone call periodically.

Use a database system that tells you which clients are invested in which areas. If something happens of significance in a particular area, give the affected client a call. If there are too many to call quickly enough, prepare a letter to all clients affected by certain events.

Call for no reason at all. Set up a system of reminders so you can call clients on birthdays or other special occasions.

Take phone calls and return phone calls. Make it a rule that no phone call goes unreturned for more than 24 hours.

Improve listening skills. Ask clients questions about what they are saying. Write down their comments. Rephrase and repeat what they say. Practice being quiet at least 50 percent of the time so the client can talk.

Do things for no fee. Do things for clients when there seems to be nothing in it for you. The rewards will come. Help enough people and money will come.

Mention clients' names. Instruct your staff and remind yourself to mention a client's name at least three times when he or she visits your office.

Know clients' habits. Have your receptionist keep a card file on the special things about the client, such as how he likes his coffee and other preferences.

Do more than is expected. If a client has an error on a transaction and you correct it, send her a small gift or thank-you note apologizing for the inconvenience and asking whether the problem was resolved to her satisfaction. Make a personal delivery of a late check or statement; go out of your way to show personal interest.

Send interesting articles. When you read something of interest to your client, copy it and send it with your card and comments. It doesn't have to be about investments.

Buy books. Send your clients complimentary copies of books that might be of interest to them about financial planning or about their industry or business.

Show appreciation for referrals. Send thank-you notes for referrals. Accompany them with tickets to the theater, complimentary dinners for two, a tree planted in the front yard, or other tokens of appreciation.

Solicit suggestions. Ask clients what you could do to make your service better. Don't ask whether you are doing all right. They will be too embarrassed to say no.

Hold appreciation events. Host an annual client appreciation night. We usually invite our clients to an annual outdoor stew. It is relatively inexpensive, considering the response we get.

Don't hide. Keep in personal touch with your clients. Don't hide behind subordinates, the computer, *The Wall Street Journal*, or any of the other myriad of excuses we use to avoid meeting clients face to face.

Keep the plan current. Keep clients' financial plans updated and refer to them consistently. Plans are the "ties that bind."

Send for Social Security benefits. Fill out a card requesting Social Security benefits and send it in for the client.

Invite service clubs. If you have room, invite service clubs to your office for lunch and a short presentation by you. They will welcome the luncheon and the program.

Invite a friend. Invite a client to a sporting event, and ask him or her to bring along a friend.

Get testimonial letters. Ask clients to write letters of referral for you.

Get an 800 number. If you have clients who must call long distance, get an 800 number to accommodate them.

Send out reminder cards for appointments.

Confirm meetings by phone.

Produce a newsletter.

Send gifts for holidays or special occasions.

Provide subscriptions to business publications.

Make house calls.

Send a thank-you note after a client makes an investment.

Offer CD rate comparison services.

Write newspaper columns, clip them and send to clients.

Give educational seminars.

Do post-tax interviews even after the sale is made.

Put a welcome sign in the lobby. Put clients' names on the sign before they arrive.

Offer new services. Provide elderly planning, estate planning, mediation, and so forth. Give clients written "helpful hints" on planning for a secure financial future.

HOW TO SECURE AND KEEP CLIENTS THROUGH SERVICE

The following ideas have been contributed by Fred Roach of the Leadership Center at Baylor Hospital, Dallas, Texas:

Know your clients. It's hard to help people you don't know. Because of your fiduciary relationship, it's critical that you know your clients very well—their dreams, objectives, and perspectives on life.

Take the initiative. Don't wait for a potential client to act—be proactive. Assume responsibility to recommend action that will be in your client's best interest.

Establish meaningful relationships. We are social beings. Relate to your client with a critical sensitivity. We usually act our best within warm relationships.

Meet both "real" and "perceived" needs. You're in a position of helping people meet needs. Some of them are real and some perceived—both are equally important.

Keep the information simple. Learn to "focus" critical issues for your client. Don't attempt to overpower with mountains of data—remember the KISS principle.

Develop your expertise. Keep learning. Let your clients know you're increasing your knowledge base—that's what they are paying for.

Keep communication open and straightforward. Stay in touch. Learn the right balance. The sharing of meaningful data indicates you are.

Take the long term into consideration. Remember that the best clients are those whom you keep for the long haul. Take their long-term interests to heart.

Create few surprises. Try not to surprise your clients—about the status of their accounts, future trends, fees, and so forth.

Really serve your client, not your financial success. Make your customers "number one." Serve their needs, be empathetic. Let the benefits flow to you from serving them well.

Form 9.1, also contributed by Fred Roach, provides a way to test your skill in establishing good client relationships.

Form 9.1 Effectiveness Test

Would You Buy from You?

The Greek philosopher Plato stated that: "The life which is unexamined is not worth living."

The English essayist and historian Thomas Carlyle said: "What we have done is the only mirror by which we can see what we are."

One of the most effective ways to assess your effectiveness in handling customers is via the question: "If you were the customer, would you buy from yourself?" You would if you scored well on the following quiz. Answer each question by checking the appropriate YES or NO blank.

	YES	NO
1. Is your image one of honest and **straightforward** sincerity?		
2. Based on your experience with customers over the past year or so, from the buyer's point of view, would you be classified as **reliable**?		
3. Could you say your customers obtained **special benefits** dealing with you they wouldn't have obtained from others?		
4. Do you think you come off as an **expert** in the eyes of your customers?		

Form 9.1 *(Continued)*

	YES	NO
5. Have you been effective in helping to solve customer problems?		
6. Wherever possible, would you say you handled customer complaints to the buyer's satisfaction?		
7. Is **integrity** one of the most important words in your vocabulary?		
8. Apart from your business dealings, do you think customers believe you have their **personal** welfare and well-being at heart?		
9. Can you honestly say most of your company's customers think of you as a **friend** as well as a business associate?		
10. Do customers look upon you as a good reliable **source** of product and industry information?		
11. Has doing business with you contributed **positively** to most of your customers' **profit performance**?		
12. Would most of your company's customers continue dealing with you even if a competitor approached them with a price that's a little bit lower?		
TOTAL NUMBER OF YES ANSWERS		

Your rating: Multiply the sum of your YES answers by 5. If you achieved a score of 55 or higher, it's a privilege to do business with you; 50 is well above average, 40 to 45 is mediocre to fair.

THE NEXT STEP

You now know:

How to use TOPS.
How to find your niche and design a marketing plan.
How to sell during tax season.
How to arrange your office and use the proper equipment and tools.
How to sell from the financial plan.
How to use mailers and tangible sales aids.
How to market to small businesses.

How to use seminars.

How to prospect.

How to service after the sale.

What are you waiting for? Stop procrastinating. Stop regarding pro-crastination as harmless. You must overcome this deadly enemy or it will overcome you. Don't let things like mailers, brochures, and so forth give you an excuse for not getting person-to-person with your client. Remember that these are "C" activities. "B" activities are seminars and the like. "A" activities are one-on-one with your clients.

Don't duck selling because you perceive it as difficult. The rewards are far greater than the small price.

PART 2

Products

TABLE OF CONTENTS

10

Selecting and Selling the Perfect Product

THE PERFECT PRODUCT

If you have read thus far, you know that I have said repeatedly that talking too much about products to your clients is probably a mistake. You need to be talking about solutions to problems and relief from pain. That admonition still stands. Yet most CPAs see implementation of financial plans as one thing—product. They want to cut directly to the chase: "What products am I going to be pushing at my clients?" Product is certainly an integral and very important part of the process, but not the most important and certainly not one to get hung up on. Many CPAs develop inertia looking for the perfect product.

The Perfect Product

1. Has the highest current yield.
2. Has the highest total return, as stated in the latest edition of *Money* or *Fortune*, for the last thirty days, six months, one year, three years, five years, ten years.
3. Has no commission charge but is accompanied by a personal advisor that can be called for advice and consolation at any time.
4. Is always included in the latest "hot list" of *Money* magazine as one of the 10 best places to put $10,000 today, funds that never go down, funds that always go up, all-weather funds, funds for all age groups, etc.
5. Never shows up in a newsletter promotional mailing on a cold list of products to get out of (possibly because they were on one of the hot lists).
6. Is totally liquid.
7. Is tax free or at least tax deferred.
8. Features accounts that can be opened for $25 or less.
9. Allows withdrawals to be made at any time in any amount.
10. Permits an investment to be exchanged for any other investment without tax consequences.

I have known many CPAs who were licensed for more than a year without making a single investment for their clients. They actually told me that they were trying to find the best investment products before making any recommendations. That's another way of saying they were looking for the perfect product. It's also another way of procrastinating. If they continue that search, it will be a lifetime effort. Their clients will not make investments, at least not through these CPAs, or they will make them through someone who knows that searching for the perfect investment is foolish. Don't use product search as an excuse for inaction. Your clients need your help.

Do you have to learn about products? Of course you do. Just don't approach products from a perspective of fear. We CPAs must overcome our natural inclination to be negative about virtually all products. Most are good. Almost all were designed to fill a perceived need. *Many* products are available to fit almost any need your client may have. Products are tools, and most are excellent tools that allow your clients to meet their financial dreams. Think of the financial planning process as a puzzle. If you find out what your client needs (his goals), what he has, and where he is today and prepare projections as to steps he needs to take to reach his destination, then you will have a puzzle with only a few pieces missing. Those missing pieces will be the products. The outline of their shapes should be apparent in the puzzle. All you have to do is sift through the pieces of products to find the right shapes.

WHICH PRODUCTS TO USE

What about product sponsors—the mutual fund companies with wholesalers and the insurance companies? They can be your most valuable resources for information, sales assistance, literature, seminars, and more. Use them, but don't abuse them. They will go the extra mile in assisting you to meet your client needs. In return, they expect you to consider their products when implementing your clients' plans.

I have probably not convinced you that selecting products is fairly easy. I was not easily convinced. With more than 10,000 selections to choose from, how can it be easy? The best way to proceed is first to *narrow the field*.

Focus on no more than three mutual fund families. With the help of the product sponsors, you can become very familiar with three fund families. Within those three, you can probably fill 80 to 90 percent of the product needs of your clients.

This was extremely difficult for me. I enjoy relationships with wholesalers and want to send business to all of them. I thought that I was doing my clients a disservice by not offering every product in the market. I especially did not want to be "identified" or "branded" by one product. Focusing on three fund families, however, will not brand you. At least one or two of the fund families should be fairly well known if you are just starting in the business. All three should probably be known for long-term, steady performance. They don't have to be on all the latest "hot lists," but they should have good, solid track records.

Pick one or two variable annuity products. This should be more than adequate for your needs. Try to pick one that works with one of the three fund families you are familiar with. Be sure that the insurance company is a strong one. Stability is probably more important than performance in today's market.

Select one fixed annuity. In many instances, your variable annuity sponsors will also have a fixed annuity. Don't select based on the highest rate. If you sell by yield, you will die by yield. Base your selection on product features and stability of the company.

Select one or two insurance companies for traditional life products. Try to limit your choice to one. However, your selection may not have a second-to-die provision or may have an inadequate term product, which may cause you to have to go to a second or third insurance company.

Select no more than two companies for disability. One may be for blue-collar workers and a second for professionals, for example.

Select one carrier for long-term care. We have now narrowed the list of companies you are dealing with to no more than 12 or, ideally, no more than 10. You should still have close to a hundred products to choose from. That is enough to meet all your clients' needs except for individual securities. For those, use the bond department or trading department of your broker-dealer.

PRESENTING THE PRODUCTS

Use a Plan: Have Only Dependable Horses in Your Stable

If your plan is in place, products will fit in like the missing pieces to a puzzle. You won't have to worry much about them. If you have done a reasonable job in selecting your stable of products, then you don't have any really bad ones in it. Why take the chance of having a "race horse" in your stable that is also very volatile? Just pick good horses that have good temperament. They won't bite your clients or kick you. If they are all you have to choose from, you can't make a very large mistake.

If you have used TOPS (as described earlier) and have prepared a plan, presenting a product should go smoothly after the sale is made. If the client is still product sensitive, then use the pointers given in the following paragraphs.

Know the Holdings Inside the Product

If your product includes some household names, be sure to open the prospectus and the annual report and show them to your client. You don't have to memorize every holding, because they change constantly. However, if you open the prospectus and let the client see some products with which he or she can identify, your sale will be easier.

Tell Stories

Tell success stories of clients who have held this product. Performance stories are not as effective as stories of individuals like your client who have had positive experiences with the product. For example, you may want to tell about an elderly couple who found that the husband had diabetes and their drug bill was going to go up dramatically. They were concerned about paying for the additional expenses at their current income level. In a phone call from your office, you were able to show them how they could increase their income through this product.

Don't have any stories yet? Borrow one or two from the product sponsor, who usually has some typical client situations spelled out in brochures. Don't lie to or mislead the client, of course, but you can take combinations of stories that will show the client how certain features of the product can be used in real-life situations.

Stick to the Basics of Investing

When your client becomes overconcerned with product even though you know that you have shown him or her good quality from your stable, because there is nothing but quality in it, return the client to the basics of investing. Sir John Templeton, founder of the Templeton Family of Mutual Funds and acknowledged worldwide for his investment expertise, stated his basics as follows:

1. *Invest for maximum total real return. This is return after taxes and inflation.*
2. *Invest—don't trade or speculate.*
3. *Remain flexible and open-minded about types of investments. There are times to buy stocks, bonds, sit on cash, etc.*
4. *Buy low—that may be obvious, but most clients will fight tooth and nail to buy high. They want to buy what everyone else likes today — the products on the "hot lists." Prices are low when demand is low, not when it is high.*
5. *When buying stocks, search for bargains among quality stocks. If your client is buying a mutual fund, point out the buying philosophy of the managers of the fund.*
6. *Buy value, not market trends or the economic outlook.*
7. *Diversify.*
8. *Do your homework, or hire wise experts to help you.*
9. *Monitor your investments (another good service that you will provide for your client).*
10. *Don't panic. Markets have always and will always change.*
11. *Learn from mistakes. The only way to avoid mistakes is not to invest— which is the biggest mistake of all. Forgive past errors. (If your client has lost his shirt in an earlier investment, work with him to get past it and not let it freeze him.)*
12. *Begin with silent reflection or a prayer. You can think more clearly and make fewer mistakes.*

13. *Outperforming the market is a difficult task. To do this, you must make better decisions than the professionals who manage the big institutions. Unmanaged market indexes are fully invested, whereas your mutual fund must sit on some cash and pay expenses that the big market doesn't have.*

14. *Don't think you have all the answers. Success is a process of continually seeking answers to new questions.*

15. *There's no free lunch.*

16. *Do not be fearful or negative too often. For 100 years, optimists have carried the day in the U.S. stock market.*

Own the Product Yourself

Put your money where your mouth is. You will have trouble convincing your clients to invest if you don't believe in the product yourself. One of the most powerful presentations of product is to pull out a statement from the product showing you as the owner.

11

Mutual Funds

I start with my usual caution. This chapter is not intended to be the know-all and end-all of everything you always wanted to know about mutual funds. It is intended to be very basic and possibly something you could share with a client or at least refer to in explaining mutual funds to clients.

Do clients know what mutual funds are? Ten years ago, most did not. Today, I think that a slim majority know the basic concept of pooling money of individual investors to increase buying power and the range of investment products available to them. Most do not know much more than that. It is up to us to educate them further.

WHAT ARE MUTUAL FUNDS?

A mutual fund is an investment company that pools the shareholders' money and invests it. The investments are made in accordance with pre-determined objectives outlined in a prospectus. The money can be invested in stocks, bonds, money market instruments, or a combination of these investments, also called securities. Individuals purchasing shares of a mutual fund, in effect, participate in a whole portfolio of securities. Mutual fund share prices are determined at the end of each business day by adding up the value of all the securities in the fund's portfolio after expenses, and dividing the sum by the total number of shares outstanding.

Mutual funds are referred to as *open-end* because they issue an unlimited number of shares and will repurchase them upon request. *Closed-end* funds issue limited shares and are usually sold on a stock exchange.

Front-load funds charge an up-front sales fee that ranges from 1 to 8.5 percent (although the 8.5 percent is fast becoming extinct).

Back-load funds deduct fees from your investment when you cash in your shares. These usually range from 1 to 5 percent, depending on how long you have held your shares. They usually disappear after five or six years.

Low-load funds charge an up-front sales fee, but less than the normal, and usually do not use brokers.

12-b-1 funds have no initial start-up sales charges. Continuing fees are paid to the fund company by the investor in order to pay our commissions. With most 12-b-1s, there is also a back-end surrender charge in case the customer wants to get out before the ongoing charges have been sufficient to recover the cost of the commission. These types of funds have received a lot of negative press because of the "hidden" nature of the charges. Whether the funds deserve this press is subject to interpretation. I think they are probably just marketed incorrectly. Some funds do have excessive ongoing charges. Comparing them with a front-end charge is difficult, because the comparison depends on the length of time held and the rate of return of the fund. However, a few rules of thumb might help:

1. The longer the client stays in the fund, the better the front-end fund looks.

2. Anything over 1 percent as an ongoing charge is probably a little high if the client is going to stay longer than five years.

3. Fund charges of 1 percent or less are fairly competitive with front-end loads for up to 10 years.

4. At 20 years or longer, the client is better off with a front-end fund.

A-B-C-D Shares

In a constant attempt to meet market demands, mutual fund companies are continuing to change the way that shares may be priced in terms of commissions. Most of the changes are improvements. In the early days of mutual funds, some funds had to be marketed at loads up to 50 percent. We are still recovering from those early days of overpricing. Today many mutual fund companies are offering us an alternative for pricing to meet our clients' comfort levels. In other words, we can work with our clients to determine the best way to purchase the shares. In actual practice, this may mean that brokers and planners will price the shares based on what they think will be best received by the client. The press will attack again, saying that clients are being misled. I usually try not to make commissions a point of argument with my client. They either need my help or they don't. If they do, they are going to pay for it. I refuse to be pulled into arguments about load versus no load. However, I do like having the ability to select the type of pricing best suited to my client's tendency to stay long-term, risk profile, sales resistance, and so forth. The key concerns are always these:

Will the client be better off with this investment or not?

What counts is how much money the client has left after all fees, not how much he paid in fees.

A shares. These carry a standard front-end load.

B shares. These have a sliding contingent deferred sales charge, that is, they are back-end loaded.

C shares. The definition varies according to the mutual fund company you are dealing with, but these usually have a low or no front load, a low or no deferred load if sold before a specified period of time, and pay a trail commission of 1 percent or so to the representative. Some are offered only to institutional accounts. In this case, there is usually no trail commission paid to the representative, but a small 1 percent fee up front.

D shares. These shares pay an annual fee of 1 percent to representatives, with no front or back load to the client.

I like the concept of D shares—100 percent of the client's money will go to work instantly. We will not get as much money up front, but we will get paid to manage the money and to keep it invested.

Most of the different types of shares are tracked separately by mutual fund companies, but will convert to regular shares after a certain period of time, usually after all contingent deferred sales charges go away.

NAV or POP

NAV stands for net asset value. It describes the true value of each share in a mutual fund, determined by adding up the value of all the securities in the fund after expenses and dividing by the number of shares outstanding.

POP stands for public offering price. This price includes the commission.

Why do we have NAV and POP? I'm not sure how the system developed, but I think I know the purpose it serves today. Having both is similar to marketing any type of security. The commission doesn't jump out and grab the customer by the throat if it is included in the POP. The customer will notice a drop in share price on her next statement when she purchases a load fund at POP. That is determined to be preferable to showing shares purchased at NAV, then showing the commission as a separate line item on the statement and deducting it from the value in the account.

With all these types of share pricing, it is obvious that the press has created a lot of make-believe villains and monsters for the consuming public to be aware of. In its desire to create news (I can't really agree that it is a desire to protect the public), the press has made many people wary of seeking the advice they need or making any investment move at all. The securities industry and its salespeople must also take on a large share of the blame for being too product and commission-oriented and for letting the press decide how the public will be informed and how investments will be marketed. As a CPA-financial planner, you need to deal personally with the issues of getting paid and how you are going to get paid. For assistance on handling client objections, refer to Chapter 1.

TYPES OF MUTUAL FUNDS

This section is not intended to be an academic presentation of all the features, benefits, and risks involved in selecting mutual fund types. Rather, it is a general guide to the various types.

Equity-Oriented Mutual Funds

There are a number of equity-oriented mutual funds:

Aggressive Growth Funds. Invest in companies that may have substantial risk in order to have the potential for higher returns. Often used synonymously with small cap or emerging growth funds, which invest in small or start-up companies with excellent potential for growth.

Specialized or Sector Funds. Restrict their holdings to the securities of companies in a particular industry, service, or region.

Long-Term Growth Funds. Invest in companies that have a chance for capital appreciation over a long period of time. Dividend income will be nominal. Often used synonymously with big cap funds.

Equity Income Funds. Invest in stocks that pay dividends so that the investor has a chance for capital appreciation as well as income. Also called growth and income funds.

Balanced Funds

Balanced funds are designed for investors seeking total return from a combination of dividends and capital appreciation. They invest in common stocks that pay dividends, preferred stocks, utility stocks, convertible bonds, and cash equivalents.

Corporate Bond Funds

Corporate bond funds invest in either high- or low-quality bonds. Some corporate bond funds invest in both, some in only high-quality. Funds that invest in low-quality bonds usually do so in order to get the yield and are called high-yield funds.

Government Securities Funds

Government securities funds invest in direct obligations of the U.S. government, such as T-bills, T-notes, T-bonds, and pass-through certificates of the Government National Mortgage Association (GNMA). They may also invest in securities backed by an agency of the U.S. government, such as the Federal Home Loan Corp. (FHLMC), (FNMA), and the Student Loan Marketing Association (SLMA).

Municipal Bond Funds

Mutual bond funds invest in bonds issued by a state, city, or local government. Interest income earned on these investments is exempt from federal taxation.

Other Types

Most other types of funds are some variation of the categories listed.

MUTUAL FUND ADVANTAGES

Explaining the advantages of mutual funds is an important part of educating your clients. The various benefits are described in the following paragraphs.

Diversification

A mutual fund invests in more securities than most individuals can afford to own. By purchasing shares in a mutual fund, you're spreading risk over a number of investments rather than just one. This keeps your client from "putting all his eggs in one basket."

Affordability

Most mutual funds have low investment minimums, making them accessible to nearly everyone.

Professional Management

Instead of taking on the time-consuming chore of choosing individual companies whose stocks or bonds are "good investments" for your client's portfolio, fund managers do this for you. Managers handle the investments in accordance with guidelines set out in the fund's prospectus. These professionals have up-to-the-minute information on trends in the financial markets, as well as in-depth data on potential investments.

Convenience

Convenience is my favorite reason for recommending mutual funds. Invariably, clients' needs change from the time of their initial investment. They may need to slightly change monthly income, withdraw a small amount of principal, add a few dollars to their account, or make some other adjustment. Using mutual funds is a convenient way to accommodate a client's varying needs.

Mutual funds provide monthly, quarterly, and annual reports. Many now provide your clients with their tax basis in the shares purchased, total returns, dividends paid, transactions made, and other figures.

Flexibility

A great advantage of mutual funds is their flexibility, which is evident in the following features:

- Most mutual funds are part of a family of funds, allowing your client to transfer portions of his or her investment into any of the other funds without incurring another commission charge.
- The investor can automatically reinvest dividends.
- The investor can automatically withdraw dividends or portions of principal.
- The investor can take portions of his or her distributions and have them sent to another mutual fund, or to another source.

- The investor can automatically do dollar cost averaging from one fund in the family to another one.

Getting Money Out

Many funds have check writing privileges; most have wire redemption privileges, direct redemption by mail, or redemption by phone.

12

Tax Exempts

One of the factors almost always listed in any client's definition of the perfect investment is tax benefit. Clients love beating the IRS. Tax-exempt municipals allow them to do that most of the time. I say most of the time because there are certain municipals that are subject to the AMT (Alternative Minimum Tax) and a rare few are even taxable.

HOW TO BUY TAX EXEMPTS

Individual Bonds

Individual bonds may be purchased for your clients by calling a broker-dealer's bond department and advising it of your client's needs and risk tolerance. The department will provide you with a list of current offerings that come closest to your targeted objectives. You generally need to act quickly, because bonds do not usually last long after being put on the market.

Advantages

1. Known maturity date.
2. Known principal and interest payment dates.
3. Only one issuer to investigate.
4. Usually readily marketable.
5. Tax basis easily tracked.
6. Easily compared with CDs.

Disadvantages

1. Can't add to your investment or partially liquidate easily.
2. Can have some principal "trickling" back to the client during the holding period. Client may not realize that the principal is being returned.
3. Risk is 100 percent in one issuer.
4. Events relating to the bond may not reach you as advisor until too late to take needed action (call announcements, downgrading of rating, etc.).
5. Can't adjust income to meet client's changing needs.

Unit Investment Trusts

I describe unit investment trusts (UITs) to my clients as a closed box of bonds with a nice ribbon around it. I contrast this with a mutual fund, which is an open box where bonds are bought and sold regularly. UITs are "packages" of several bonds that are bought by an investment management company which markets "units" of the trust (usually in denominations of $1,000 to $5,000).

Advantages

1. Fixed payments of principal and interest.
2. Call provisions available from packaging company.
3. Information on status of municipalities available.
4. Known maturity dates, although there may be several.
5. Most allow automatic reinvestment of principal or interest or both into a mutual fund family.
6. Risk spread over several issues.

Disadvantages

1. May involve yield to maturity, yield to call, and estimates of total return based on unknown factors.
2. Not as easy to liquidate as a mutual fund.
3. May have to explain different initial payments to the client because of accrued interest in the purchase price, buying between payment dates, etc.
4. Principal "trickle in" may not be understood by client, and he or she may fail to reinvest.
5. Can't adjust income to meet client's changing needs.
6. Tracking tax basis can be difficult if principal distributions are erratic.

Mutual Funds

Mutual funds are explained in general terms in Chapter 11. They are also one of the ways that tax exempt securities may be purchased.

Advantages

1. Risk spread over many issuers.
2. Flexibility in investing, income distribution, and withdrawals. Can adjust to meet client's changing needs. Allow for minimal investments and withdrawals, changes in income distributions, etc.
3. Tax basis may be provided by mutual fund company.
4. Professional management.
5. Affordability.

Disadvantages

1. No known maturity date (client cannot say for sure when he or she is going to get his or her money back), because there are so many issues in the fund and they may be actively traded.

2. Client may not identify with a mutual fund share as readily as he or she does with a bond certificate.
3. Client may pay taxes on gains taken in the fund and distributed to him or her.
4. Funds look less like a CD to a client who understands only CDs.

TAX EXEMPTS (MUNICIPALS) AND TAXES

One of the most overlooked and best sales tools around is the use of tax-able equivalent yield and its cousin, "after-tax net." Most financial advisors use taxable equivalent yield to wow their clients, but the clients may not have the foggiest notion of what they are talking about. They often buy only because the investment is tax free. In today's financial environment, taxable equivalent yield is not as meaningful as it usually is, because tax-exempt yields are already as much as or more than taxable yields on CDs. It doesn't take a client long to figure out that this may be a good deal. However, this situation is temporary, and we must learn how to use all the tools at our disposal while explaining that munis (municipals) are not without risk.

Taxable Equivalent Yield

It's what you keep that counts, correct? Show your clients the current tax-exempt yield on bonds. Convert that rate to a taxable equivalent rate as follows:

Tax-exempt rate 5%
Tax rate 28%

Taxable Equivalent Yield

$$1.00 \text{ less tax rate } .28 = .72$$

$$5\% \text{ divided by } .72 = 6.944\%$$

Test your work as follows:

$$6.944\% \text{ less } 28\% = 5.00\%$$

Explain to your client that she would have to have a 6.944 percent CD to keep as much money as she will with a 5 percent tax exempt. Then convert the illustration into at least a $100,000 CD, even if you are talking about only $10,000. The importance of the difference will be more apparent to the client if you use $100,000 rather than $10,000.

After-Tax Net

After-tax net is just as effective as the taxable equivalent yield and easier for most clients to comprehend quickly. It is easy to calculate by subtracting taxes from the current CD rate.

CD or equivalent investment rate	5%
Tax rate	31%
Net rate on CD	3.45%

Clients can readily see that they are keeping only 3.45 percent. Subtract an inflation rate of 3 percent from 3.45 percent, and the client is getting a "real rate of return" of .45 percent.

If the client is still not convinced, use an illustration like that found in Table 12.1. Don't use a preprinted table to show these numbers! Calculate them right in front of your client on a grease board or a yellow pad. In today's economy, these numbers will be even more dramatic, because tax-exempt yields often exceed taxable yields on CDs.

There are three types of munis created by the Tax Reform Act of 1986:

1. *The true tax exempt.* Less than 10 percent of the proceeds is for private use and security, and less than 5 percent is used for loans to nongovernmental persons; that is, the proceeds are predominantly used for public purposes or a 501(c)(3) qualified security.

2. *Private activity.* These munis are used by exempt facilities, such as multifamily housing, airports, wharves, mass transit, sewage, solid waste, electricity, gas, water, hydro, heating and cooling, and hazardous waste.

   Other exemption qualifications include small issue Industrial Development Bonds, student loans, mortgage revenue, and redevelopment. These will be tax exempt but will be considered preference items for the AMT.

Table 12.1 Comparison of Yields

	Taxable Investment	Tax-Exempt Investment
Amount	$100,000	$100,000
Yield	6%	5%
Income Annually	$6,000	$5,000
Taxes at 31%	(1,860)	(0)
Net	$4,140	$5,000
*Value in 10 Years	$150,029	$162,889
Difference		$12,860

*Assumes no fluctuation in principal and all income reinvested.

3. If none of the exemptions are met, then the bond is considered for private purposes and will be taxable.

In addition to the preceding qualifications, a distinction must be made between those tax exempts whose carrying costs can be deducted by banks and thrifts (at an 80 percent rate) and those whose carrying costs cannot be deducted. The determining factor is whether the issuer expects to issue less than $10 million in tax-exempt debt during the current calendar year. If the issuer is issuing more than $10 million in a year and bank carrying costs are 80 percent deductible, then they are not tax exempt. If the bank carrying costs are not deductible, then tax exempt status still applies.

Sound complicated? This information is relatively easy to understand when investing in munis by any of the three methods. Don't decide to avoid bonds subject to AMT altogether. They usually pay a quarter to a half percentage point more than other bonds, and less than 1/20th of 1 percent of the population pays the AMT.

TAX EXEMPTS VS. NONDEDUCTIBLE IRAS

I have found that doing calculations comparing tax-free investments with tax-deferred investments, such as IRAs and annuities, adds some sizzle for clients who have primarily invested in CDs. Many will argue about the need to "pay as they go." Since you are going to have to pay taxes on the money sometime, why put it off? Again, don't use a table to show the client. Make a customized presentation using your grease board and your financial calculator.

Assuming your client is now 39 and plans to take his IRA at 59, Table 12.2 gives an example of such a calculation.

Most clients will not remove their IRAs all at once. Interest rates will change, as can other circumstances. But this type of illustration done before the client's eyes, based on his age and additional factors, will contribute greatly to his education and can assist him in making an educated decision about whether he wants to invest in a nondeductible IRA.

Table 12.2 Comparison of IRA and Tax Exempt

	Nondeductible IRA	Tax Exempt	
Annual Investment	$2,000	$2,000	
Rate of Return	6%	5%	
Annual Tax	none	none	
Value in 20 Years	$77,985	$69,438	
Tax Rate	33%	33%	
Tax If Withdrawn	$25,735	$0	
Net Remaining	$52,250	$69,438	
Difference			$17,188

Table 12.3   Moody's Bond Ratings

Description of Rating	Grade
Loans are of the best quality, enjoying strong protection from established cash flows of funds for their servicing, or from established and broad-based access to the market or refinancing, or both.	MIG 1
Loans are of high quality, with margins of protection ample, although not as large as in the top-rated group.	MIG 2
Loans are of favorable quality, with all security elements accounted for, but lacking the undeniable strength of the preceding grades. Market access for refinancing, in particular, is likely to be less well established.	MIG 3
Loans are of adequate quality, carrying specific risk but having protection commonly regarded as required of an investment security and not distinctly or predominantly speculative.	MIG 4

SAFETY OF TAX EXEMPTS

The default rate on munis is about three-tenths of 1 percent over the last 50 years. However, that doesn't mean that there is no risk. If your client's bond happens to fall within that .3 percent, the pain is just as great as with a riskier investment.

Insurance or Not?

I usually don't buy insured bonds if I am buying through a UIT or mutual fund personally. However, I do have several clients who like the insurance. It comes with a cost ranging around 10 to 50 basis points, but if it makes your client comfortable, I recommend it. The muni market is very fragmented now, and rating services may not be current for an issuer. In addition, brokerage houses have very limited inventories for munis. When supply dries up, there is usually a lot of demand for insured issues.

Rating Services

Rating services can be helpful in deciding on which bonds to purchase. Moody's, one of many, rates bonds as shown in Table 12.3.

Nonrated bonds can be good buys. Many fairly strong issuers may just not want to pay for a rating. However, unless you know something about the nonrated issuer, it is probably best to keep your risk-averse clients away from these issues. If such bonds are bought, they should probably be part of a portfolio in a mutual fund that also holds some rated bonds.

How about interest rate risk? Long-term munis fluctuate with changes in interest rates in similar fashion to other bonds.

13

Taxable Income Instruments

CORPORATE BONDS

Corporate bonds are issued by corporations as a way for them to borrow money from investors, rather than banks. They are sold in denominations of $1,000 each. They usually pay a fixed amount of interest and have a fixed maturity date. Bondholders are creditors whose claims must be satisfied before stockholders upon liquidation of the company.

The major types of corporate bonds are as follows:

1. Mortgage bonds—secured by real estate.
2. Equipment trust certificates—secured by specific equipment.
3. Debentures—unsecured; supported by the creditworthiness of the issuing corporation.

Corporate bonds can be purchased individually (usually in units of at least $10,000), as part of unit investment trusts (UITs), or in mutual funds. All three methods were discussed earlier in Chapter 12 on tax exempts. Their advantages and disadvantages are also the same.

Moody's and Standard & Poor's rate all corporate bonds. They have their own letter codes for quality (e.g., AAA, BB, or C, with AAA being the highest for Standard & Poor's, and AAA the highest for Moody's).

Check to see how senior a bond is to other bonds issued by the company. Is the bond callable? Be sure that your bond offers at least five years of payments before the issuing company can call it in.

GOVERNMENT BONDS

Government bonds are quite similar to corporate bonds, except that they are issued by the U.S. government. Treasury bonds are backed by the full faith and credit of the U.S. government; they are also free from state income tax.

T-bills, notes, and bonds are direct debt of the U.S. Treasury, but maturities are under five years for t-bills and notes and over five years for bonds, respectively.

The Government National Mortgage Association (GNMA, or Ginnie Mae) is also part of the federal government. Its securities are backed by the full faith and credit of the U.S. government. Essentially, a purchaser's investing in a pool of mortgages put together by the agency. The mortgages are mostly for single-family home owners.

When mortgages are prepaid or refinanced, payment is apportioned to the certificate holders on a pro rata basis and may cause your client investor's principal to "trickle in," unnoticed by the client.

Risk. How can there be risk in an investment backed by the full faith and credit of the good old U.S.A.? Putting aside the matter of the burgeoning national deficit, the risk involved is a function of interest rates.

Purchasing a long-term U.S. government security has the same interest rate risk as purchasing a long-term municipal or a long-term corporate bond.

ZERO COUPON BONDS

Zero coupon bonds (zeros) became available in 1981 when U.S. Treasury bonds were split into their principal and interest components and sold separately. When you buy a zero, you actually own a bond's interest coupon, reissued as a new security, that will be paid out in a lump sum at maturity. That means that there are no semiannual interest payments as there are with other bonds. Maturity dates could occur within a few months or in as much as 30 years. There are zero versions of Treasury, government agency, corporate, and municipal bonds.

Target Market

A CPA's target market for zero coupon bonds includes:

- Investors saving for retirement.
- Parents putting money away for their children's or grandchildren's college education.
- Speculators betting on interest rate shifts.

Note the widely divergent market. Zero coupon Treasuries, for example, have appeal to the very conservative investor who wants the assurance that a certain, predetermined amount will be paid to him or her at a predetermined time. Because long-term zeros fluctuate at roughly twice the rate of conventional bonds, they also appeal to speculators betting on interest rate swings. The wider swing in values is due to interest not being paid out until maturity. Interest is reinvested at the same rate. With conventional bonds, interest is paid out semiannually and can be reinvested at the new rates. However, investors in zeros do not incur reinvestment risk.

The appeal of zero coupon bond lies, first, in the high, guaranteed return if they are held until maturity. Particularly with Treasuries, investors are guaranteed to get their investment back if these are held until maturity.

Another attractive feature of zeros is a low price, a fraction of the typical bond's $1,000 face value. Investors like owning a zero with a face of $100,000 and possibly paying only $20,000 for it. It makes them feel secure and richer than they really are.

In assessing zero coupon bonds for risk, keep in mind that principal fluctuations are worse than for other bonds, as detailed earlier. But that can also mean great opportunity for gains. Check the ratings and use the same precautions you would with any other bond investment. Be sure to ask whether the zero is callable and determine both the yield to maturity and the yield to call. Try to buy only noncallable for your conservative clients.

CMOs

Collateralized Mortgage Obligations (CMOs) were introduced in the early 1980s to help minimize the reinvestment and interest rate risks of standard mortgage-backed securities such as Ginnie Maes. Collateralized mortgage obligations take the cash flows from a number of mortgage-backed securities and then split them into a group of bonds with different maturities. Most of these bond classes receive interest from the mortgages—the collateral. But principal repayments go first to the class with the shortest maturity. When these bonds are retired, the principal is channeled to the bonds with the next shortest maturity. The process continues until all classes are paid off.

A dozen maturity classes, called *tranches* (from the French for ''slice'') is the norm today. Instead of one security with a stated final maturity of 15 to 30 years, there may be classes with final maturities estimated at 3 years, 5 years, 10 years, and so on. But the prepayment risk isn't entirely eliminated, so CMOs command higher yields relative to gilt-edged bonds, such as Treasury issues.

The appeal of CMOs was expanded by the introduction of the Real Estate Mortgage Investment Conduit (REMIC) security in 1987. REMICs offer preferred tax treatment of both issuers and investors. REMICs are structured into classes with different interest rates, average lives, prepayment sensitivities, and maturities. Investors can select the class that best fits their needs.

REMIC interests, both regular and residual, are treated as qualifying real estate assets for thrifts and real estate investment trusts (REITs) seeking to meet applicable tax qualification requirements.

CMOs make monthly interest and principal payments. The interest is subject to both state and federal income taxes.

14

Equities

The case for equities (stocks) is so overwhelming that I will not attempt to improve on what has already been said. Some of the best marketing material for any profession is available from product sponsors and other sources, stating the history of the market since inception. Use these resources. Put up displays in your office.

In an equity investment, the investor takes an ownership position in an asset or business. The return is based on the demand for that asset or business, so there are various degrees of risk involved. Over time, these have generally proved to be rewarding investments and excellent inflation hedges.

DEALING WITH FEAR

Many registered representatives deal with fear by avoiding it. If their clients are uneducated about the stock market, they often put them into "guaranteed" government funds. In the 1980s many clients were disturbed to discover that government securities also fluctuate.

When you ask the average client what he or she thinks of when you mention risk in investments, the usual answer is "stocks." When I first began educating myself and my clients about investing and presenting a few products, they would always ask, "This is not *stock*, is it? This is insured, isn't it?" I admit to a great deal of frustration in those early days. However, I kept right on telling the story to anyone who would listen. The change occurred when I started believing myself. That's when my presentations changed from wooden and tentative to enthusiastic and confident.

How do you overcome your less sophisticated clients' nervousness about stocks? Educate, educate, educate! Have patience when you have to repeat the same story. The evidence in favor of equities is overwhelming if you can get your clients to listen. Use the same principles outlined in previous portions of this book, concentrating on the client's problems, pain, and solution. State your investment philosophy: save for the short term, invest for the long term; maintain an emergency fund; invest regularly; diversify; keep a long-term perspective.

What are the long-term results? Compare the results obtained between 1926 and 1992 from the following investment categories:

Common stocks	10.3%
Long-term government bonds	4.8%
U.S. Treasury bills	3.7%
Inflation	3.1%

Table 14.1 Inflation Over Ten Years

	1982	1992	%
Average home	$69,000	$122,000	77%
McDonald's milkshake	.80	1.39	74%
Paperback book	3.30	6.45	95%
Man's haircut	8.00	14.00	75%
First-class stamp	.20	.29	45%
Ice cream cone	.85	1.79	110%

INVESTING FOR REAL RETURNS

Clients should be educated to invest for total return after taxes and inflation. It is vital to protect purchasing power. One of the biggest mistakes that people make is putting too much money into fixed income securities. If inflation averages 4 percent, it will reduce the buying power of $100,000 to $68,000 in just 10 years. Show your clients how prices have increased over time, as in Table 14.1.

WHEN TO INVEST

From the beginning, clients have been giving me excuses about timing. They ask, "Do you think that now is a good time to invest?" It is revealing to look back over history at the so-called wrong times to invest. There have always been and will continue to be problems with investing. There are very few, if any, times when all signals are right for investing. During those times, most people will not invest because investing is not popular just then. The answer to clients who ask when is a good time, is "Now" or "Anytime." History has shown that despite short-term fluctuations that include high and low periods, the financial markets have provided investors with outstanding long-term growth. History also tells us that it is wise to be in the market during upturns.

INVESTMENT STRATEGY

With dollar cost averaging (DCA), your client invests a fixed amount of money at regular intervals. If share prices go up, this fixed amount will purchase fewer shares. If prices go down, the fixed amount will buy more shares. Through the use of this strategy, more shares will be accumulated at a lower average cost.

Teach your clients that trying to outguess the market is futile. Timing doesn't work. Advise them to relax and let their investments work for them. Moreover, an investor should be contrarian: buy when demand is low. They should buy when all their friends and colleagues are selling.

In planning a total investment strategy, keep in mind that stocks also enjoy some tax benefits. Growth is not taxed until the investor sells the stock or investment in the mutual fund. Capital gains still enjoy a maximum rate that is lower than the maximum tax rate.

15

Annuities

During the early years of my CPA practice, I was a big deal-killer on annuity sales. Whenever clients asked my advice about an annuity purchase, I usually took the easy way out and advised against it. Why? Because annuities were not as good in those days as they are today. However, the primary reason was that I had read most of the available information on annuities, and it was largely negative. The primary complaint? You give up control when you annuitize. Today, annuities are a large part of my practice because they fit certain needs of clients and they have many benefits. They are also probably one of the easiest products on the market to sell. Consider some of the advantages.

Advantages

1. Tax-deferred earnings.
2. Very similar to CDs.
3. Interest and principal payments guaranteed by the insurance company for the fixed portion of the contract (and by a state guarantee fund, in some states, up to certain limits).
4. Various options for taking money out. Some products offer as many as 15 ways to take distributions.
5. Guaranteed lifetime income option available.
6. With variable annuities, a choice of a guaranteed investment or a variable investment with a chance for growth.
7. Guaranteed death benefit in almost all contracts for variable annuities. If the annuitant dies before payments have begun and the variable account is lower than the cost, the beneficiary is guaranteed to receive no less than 100 percent of the purchase payments.
8. No dollar limits, as there are with IRAs.
9. No mandatory distribution at age 70-1/2 unless the annuity is in a qualified plan.
10. Protection from creditors.
11. Telephone switching (just call the insurance company and change your investments from one variable fund to another) in variable annuities available on most products.
12. Automatic dollar cost averaging available in some products if the investor wants to increase potential return while minimizing risks.
13. No maturity date problem and interest rate negotiation, as there are with CDs.
14. Rates competitive with CDs, usually exceeding them by 25 to 150 basis points.
15. Privacy: annuities don't even show up on the investor's tax return.
16. Exclusion of earnings in determining whether Social Security benefits will be taxed.

17. (For most annuities) 10% withdrawal privileges each year without any deferred sales charge.
18. Affordability: most flexible premium annuities will accept $25. Other annuities require an initial investment of $1,000 to $10,000.
19. Many investment options available with variable annuities.
20. Withdrawals permitted without penalty for death, disability, or hardship.
21. Statements for fixed annuities given in dollars, not shares; less confusing for some clients.
22. In a variable contract, ability to switch between accounts without tax consequences.
23. Usually no front-end commission.
24. Variable accounts (because they are not assets of the insurance company) not subject to credit risk.

Of course, like any other type of investment, annuities have certain drawbacks.

Disadvantages

1. Annuities are subject to surrender charges that usually last from five to ten years.
2. Early withdrawal penalties apply before age 59-1/2 unless there is a scheduled withdrawal based on life expectancy.
3. If the contract is annuitized, the owner loses control of his or her principal.
4. Contract charges for administration of variable contracts are usually higher than for most mutual funds.
5. Mortality charges apply in variable accounts where a death benefit is offered.
6. At the investor's death, growth or earnings in excess of premiums paid is taxed as ordinary income.
7. The annuitant may be at an interest rate disadvantage at withdrawal time if interest rates are down and the annuitant wishes to annuitize.

TYPES OF ANNUITIES

Fixed vs. Variable Annuities

Fixed annuities are very similar to certificates of deposit. In explaining to clients, I compare annuities to CDs with an insurance company. The fixed annuity is simply a contract with an insurance company to pay a certain rate of interest for a specified period of time. You can assist your clients in selecting the time period that best suits their needs. It is usually easy to tell which way the insurance company feels interest rates are headed by looking at its offerings of interest rates for varying periods of time. If its rate for a five-year guarantee is less than its one-year contract, then the company thinks rates are coming down. The company wants to encourage the client to take the one-year deal so that it can renew at lower rates. If it encourages clients to lock in rates for longer periods of time, that may mean that the company feels interest rates are going up. Does the insurance company know something we don't? Probably not, but it is an interesting sales point for a client.

What happens at the end of the guarantee period? Most contracts allow the client to select another guarantee period. Some just renew at the current rate.

What happens when the guaranteed periods are used up and the surrender charge period is gone? Then the client has the option of renewing or looking at one of the withdrawal options if she is over age 59-1/2. If under 59-1/2, she can also consider a 1035 exchange.

Variable annuities could be one of the most flexible and multipurpose products on the market today. They are probably not going to be the highest performers for a specific purpose (although performance can certainly be outstanding), but they do meet many investor goals.

Variable contracts combine the features of the fixed annuity with the flexibility of a group of mutual funds. The client can allocate his money to a fixed account and to a group of mutual funds (choices usually range from five to nine). He can switch from one account to another without tax implications.

Variable accounts are not assets of the insurance company and thus not subject to creditors' claims. Since no mutual fund company has ever failed, this can give some comfort to your clients who are worried about insurance companies. Some variable accounts are managed by a mutual fund company separate from the insurance company, others are managed by a company that is owned by the insurance company.

Flexible vs. Single Premium Annuities

Some contracts will accept only single premiums of a certain minimum. Most minimums are $5,000. Others will accept periodic regular payments. A bank draft plan or a retirement plan contract may be required.

Immediate vs. Deferred Annuities

Immediate annuities start paying income immediately. You should be sure that your client has other assets before committing to an immediate annuity. In addition, check with two or three companies to determine who has the best distribution based on the option selected by your client. Just because your client is invested in an immediate annuity and is drawing income does not necessarily mean that the contract is "annuitized" in the usual definition of that term. Annuitization usually means that a portion of the client's principal is being distributed to him with each payment and that the distribution option is fixed and unchangeable. Most immediate annuities, however, are "annuitized." Once the client selects an option, it is permanent.

ANNUITY FEATURES AND OPTIONS

Surrender Charges

Surrender charges are sometimes called contingent deferred sales charges (CDSC). The specter of "tying your money up" is in a close race with worries about insurance company safety as the number one deterrent to annuity sales. Surrender charges are usually "plain vanilla" percentages paid by the client who takes money out before the surrender period is up. However, there are certain misconceptions in clients' minds that should be addressed.

- Most contracts guarantee that you will never get less than your original investment back. Clients are usually concerned about losing their principal.
- Even in contracts that will take part of your principal, they usually have a clause that says that you can withdraw in the first year without losing any of your original investment. If you get past the first year, most interest earnings are going to be adequate to keep you from getting anything less than the amount of your original investment back. Moreover, the surrender penalties begin declining in the second year.
- Check to see whether the sales charge applies to both principal and accumulated interest. Most apply to principal only.
- Check to see whether the contract begins a new surrender period every time new money is deposited. In a number of 403(b) accounts, for example, many insurance companies start a new period every month; that is, the client never gets totally past the surrender period. The contract should start a surrender period with the first deposit and protect all future deposits within this same time period.
- Most surrender charges are waived in the event of disability or death.

Withdrawal Rights

Most contracts allow your client to withdraw 10 percent of the contract once each year without incurring any surrender charges. This will not protect the client from the IRS, however.

Loan Provisions

Many contracts have a loan provision that allows the contract owner to borrow at 2 percent net interest. In other words, the company will charge 2 percent more on the borrowed funds than it pays for the money on deposit. Loan provisions are usually found in 403(b) and 401(k) contracts.

Commissions

Most annuities have no front-end commission, so that all of the clients money goes to work from the time of the investment. The insurance representative is paid a previously specified rate, depending on the contract.

Death Benefit

Most variable annuities have a mortality feature often referred to as the "die in a down market" clause. If your client dies before annuity payments begin, the beneficiary will receive no less than the original purchase payments made plus any earnings realized.

Withdrawal Options

Withdrawal options require your close scrutiny with the client and represent one of the major sales points we make to our clients to get them to select our products. Clients will need consultation at time of withdrawal. The following are summary descriptions of a few common withdrawal options. Many contracts have as many as 15 options, but most are some variation of these:

Interest Only—Allows the client to withdraw interest only.

Straight Life or Lifetime Only—Pays the client until she dies, no matter how short or how long that time is. If she dies too soon, the insurance company will get to keep some of her investment. Since there is that risk, this option comes with the highest monthly payment.

A Life and Period Certain—Pays the client and his beneficiary for at least a specified number of years (period certain), typically 10, 15, or 20 years. This guarantees that either the client or his beneficiary will receive payments for the certain period of time selected. Benefits are usually 5 to 8 percent less than with the straight life option.

Installment Refund—Pays back the client's original investment to his beneficiary if he dies. This option usually pays 4 to 5 percent less than the straight life option.

Cash-Refund Annuity—Works like the installment refund option, except that the survivor receives the balance of the original investment in a lump sum.

Joint and Survivor—Pays until the client and spouse are dead. The amount of the benefit is based on both ages. Survivor benefit can also be reduced by 25, 33, or 50 percent if the client so selects. This can also be combined with the period certain option.

Lump Sum—Pays a lump sum value in the contract. This option is not often used because of the tax consequences. The remainder after taxes will seldom produce the same income as one of the other options.

SELECTING ANNUITY PROVIDERS

The selection of annuity products is very similar to the selection of any investment product, especially one offered through an insurance company. You need products that are competitive and flexible enough to meet your clients' changing needs.

Features to look for when selecting an annuity product might include:

1. Strength of the insurance company.
2. Severity of surrender charges and length of the surrender period.
3. Whether surrender charges apply to the entire contract value or to just the principal invested.
4. Options on retirement. This is probably one of the most important concerns. Are there an adequate number of options available for withdrawal of the client's money?
5. Liberal (and usually without cost) transfer privileges within the variable accounts.
6. A low annual maintenance fee or a guarantee that it will never increase.
7. No initial sales charge.
8. How commissions are paid to you and whether there is a trail (an ongoing small management fee paid to the Registered Representative—usually 25 basis points).
9. Availability of automatic dollar cost averaging.
10. Minimum investment required, and the flexibility of subsequent premiums.
11. Availability of loan provisions.
12. Frequency of account statements. Some are only annual; ask for quarterly.
13. Automatic asset allocation. Some clients will automatically rebalance your accounts in the variable side.
14. Annual withdrawal privileges.
15. Past performance in the variable accounts.
16. Wide range of investment options.

17. Interest rate history in fixed accounts as compared with T-bill or CD rates.

DOES TAX DEFERRAL REALLY PAY?

Many clients would prefer to pay as they go, rather than run the risk of tax rates heading up and paying at higher rates at retirement. It is hard to argue against the possibility that tax rates might go up. Moreover, many annuity buyers intend to make just as much money, if not more, in retirement than they did during their working years. Does tax deferral then pay off? I have often compared tax deferred investments with tax-free and taxable investments in client meetings. This works very effectively. Start with an open mind as to which will win in various situations. You should tell the client that you do not know what the outcome will be. Let the client pick the interest rates and tax rates and then do the comparison right in front of him or her. After doing this several times over the years, I concluded that tax deferral is much more powerful than I originally thought. If the client stays in an investment for five years or longer, deferral usually pays off. The results, of course, depend on the variance in the rate of return and the tax rates used. However, clients almost always wind up with more money under tax deferral if the holding period is 10 years or more. Learn to do these calculations well enough so that you can do them with the client watching. They are much more powerful when calculated before the client's eyes.

MARKETING ANNUITIES

As indicated earlier in this chapter, I have found annuities to be one of the easiest investment products to market. They are easy for clients to understand because they are similar to CDs and have some excellent benefits.

The Liquidity Objection

Overcoming the liquidity objection is usually fairly easy once you get over it yourself. The most effective way to persuade a client is through the following steps:

Use illustrations showing that taking the money out is not as bad as it seems.

Point out the differences between CDs and annuities. Relate the surrender penalties to early withdrawal penalties.

Show the client that most products never allow the client to lose principal.

Show the various ways to take money out.

The Treasure Chest

Most annuity prospects have funds that are not being used and are not needed for liquidity. Draw treasure chests for your client. One or more chests may contain funds that meet certain needs, such as income. Show that chest with the top open. Illustrate money coming out for living expenses and so forth. Also show the IRS dipping its hand into the chest annually for its share of the money. Then draw a chest with a lock on it. That's the annuity. The client can push the IRS hand away until he or she is ready to withdraw money. The exercise may be rather simple, but it works.

The Umbrella

I am not an artist, but I do use my grease board to illustrate certain points because I believe that most people are visual learners. One of the most effective ways I have found to educate clients about variable annuities is with an umbrella. I draw an umbrella on the grease board and show some rain falling. The rain represents taxes, and the umbrella represents the variable annuity.

On the left side of the umbrella, I draw a single box which represents the fixed portion of the variable annuity. I explain that this is like a guaranteed investment contract with an insurance company or a CD with an insurance company. On the right side, I draw several boxes representing the mutual fund options for the variable side. I may put amounts in the boxes, but usually I just show the client's ability to switch around between the boxes without incurring any tax liability.

Prospects for Annuities

There are certain clients who are very good prospects for annuities:

- Clients who have substantial funds invested in taxable instruments for liquidity purposes.
- School teachers and all employees of 501(c)(3) organizations.
- Clients who own taxable mutual funds.
- Anyone who has a tax problem.
- Clients who have nondeductible IRAs.
- Clients who own any taxable bond or taxable bond mutual funds, especially government funds.
- Clients past 50 years of age who are accumulating funds for retirement.
- Retired clients with tax problems.

- Clients whose Social Security benefits are being taxed.
- Clients who like to manage their mutual funds actively but would like to avoid the tax consequences of trading.

Clients can use annuities to fund the premium on long-term care contracts by using the 10 percent penalty-free withdrawal available every year. The client is thus protected against the single largest threat to his or her assets while those assets continue to grow without taxation.

16

Insurance Products

Like mutual funds, insurance products are in abundance. But for accountants, they are more difficult to understand, because the terms used vary from one product to another. Moreover, the insurance industry has grown up behind a façade of marketing terms that fail to describe the ways things really are. Today, for example, the American Society of Certified Life Underwriters (CLU) and Chartered Financial Consultants (ChFC) has developed an insurance illustration questionnaire (IQ) described as being "on the cutting edge of a major industry concern" and is said to be "leading a quiet revolution dealing with a major industry concern—responsible use of life insurance application illustrations during the sales process."

The Illustration Questionnaire

The IQ is a series of questions designed to help life insurance agents gather specific information from their companies regarding assumptions used in generating life insurance sales illustrations. The premise is to learn from insurance companies what assumptions are used in illustrations regarding:

Mortality
Interest or Crediting Rates
Expenses
Persistency

If the agent knows these things, he should be better able to help clients make informed decisions about how the policy being proposed helps meet their objectives. The IQ is new, so don't expect immediate and positive industry reaction. However, the following IQ questions can help you to evaluate illustrations for your clients.

INSURANCE PRODUCTS

Basic

These are some questions you should probably ask of the insurance company or the person who is assisting you in making a client presentation.

1. Is the policy participating or non-participating?
2. Describe any non-guaranteed elements in the proposal.
3. Describe what is guaranteed in the proposal.
4. Do the underlying experience factors for any non-guaranteed elements differ from current experience? If they do, please describe.
5. Is there a substantial probability that the current illustrated values will change if current experience continues unchanged?

6. Are new and existing policyholders treated the same with regard to pricing?

Mortality

1. Are mortality rates used lower than recent company experience (five years)?
2. Are improvement in mortality rates assumed?
3. Do mortality rates vary by product?

Interest or Crediting Rates

1. How is the interest rate determined? (i.e., is it gross or net of expenses, etc.).
2. Does the rate exceed the current earning rate on the company's investments that back this group of policies?
3. Does the interest rate vary by policy duration? By product?
4. Do the interest rates include capital gains?

Expenses

1. Do expenses used reflect recent company experience? For what period? If not, how did you arrive at the expense charges?
2. Are expense determinations consistently determined for new as well as existing policies?
3. Do the expenses vary by product?

Persistency

1. If actual persistency is better than assumed, would illustrated values be less?
2. Persistency bonuses are paid or credited to all policyholders who pay premiums for a minimum for a specified number of years. Are bonuses included in the illustrations?

But what does the CPA-planner do while terms and illustrations are being developed? Do we wash our hands of insurance products because the industry has problems with illustrations? Give up and leave it to insurance agents? We must continue to meet our client needs in this area. Insurance planning is part of the financial planning process just as estate planning is. You can't do an effective job for your clients without knowing about this area. This does not mean that you can't make an investment for a client without including insurance or an estate plan, it just means that you must be able to deal with these issues because clients do have needs in this area.

How do you effectively deal with insurance products?

1. *Limit the number of companies you deal with.* Stick with companies that have long histories of customer service, high ratings, and meeting projections.

2. *Limit your products.* It isn't necessary to know every last detail about every product, but you should know how illustrations are prepared, what needs the product is supposed to fill, and so forth.

3. *Learn by doing.* Inertia is still your greatest enemy. You must start using illustrations in your analysis of insurance products in real-life client situations. You will never learn unless you begin.

4. *Use the competition.* Look at competitors' illustrations and compare theirs with yours, item by item. Look at illustrations for other products within the same company. Get your insurance department to explain why one product is better than another. Look also at other companies that you are appointed to do business with. Ask for their solutions to the same customer need. Then you can show the client that you have investigated more than one product to fit his or her needs and, more important, why you selected the one you did.

5. *Ask dumb questions.* We CPAs are used to being on the receiving end of questions. We don't ask questions, we answer them. Swallow your pride, make a commitment to learn for the sake of your clients, and don't be afraid to say, "I don't know." Then find out by asking all the people and checking all the resources you can find. From each of these fact-finding missions, you will become a little more astute in this area. Working with client situations is always the best way to learn.

6. *Use plain-language cover sheets for presentations.* Most insurance illustrations will not help you to sell the product. That is doubly true if you don't completely understand the illustration. Focus on the key points you want to achieve for your client. Find where these are shown on the illustration and highlight them for the client. We find it helpful to prepare a cover sheet explaining in simple language the various components of the illustration.

7. *Use an "Insurance Illustration Caution" cover sheet.* We use the cover sheet shown in the box below to explain how the insurance illustration process is often abused.

INSURANCE ILLUSTRATION CAUTION

It is often said that an insurance professional had better be the "first and only" or the last person to prepare an insurance illustration. Unfortunately, this is true. If given the opportunity, we can also beat any competitive quote. This is true not only because we have a variety of insurance companies and products to choose from, but an infinite variety of "assumptions" that we can make regarding future interest rates and other factors.

> What does this mean to you, the consumer? It means that you must ask each professional you are dealing with what assumptions were made to arrive at the numbers in your illustration. The cheapest policy is not always the best policy! Be sure that your insurance professional has made realistic assumptions that are in your best interest. Always deal with professionals whom you know and trust.
>
> We have prepared the attached illustrations using the best information available to meet your financial goals.

8. *Use "outside" services.* Services such as INSMARK have developed a great business by capitalizing on the insurance industry's inability to speak English. Such programs prepare better illustrations using the insurance company products than the insurance company can produce on its own.

9. *Make your insurance illustrations goal oriented.* Develop narrative and numbers that tie into the illustration but also focus on what has to be done to reach the client's goals. Remember, people don't buy life insurance, they buy what it does for them.

WHOLE LIFE

Also known as straight life and ordinary life. It usually provides insurance protection at a level premium for the lifetime of the insured. Thus the term *whole* life. Premiums pay for the client's insurance and administrative costs as well as funding a cash value account.

Many whole life policies also earn insurance company dividends (if they are participating) that add to the cash value. Such dividends often exceed the premium in later years and the client can use the dividends to pay his premiums.

This product is primarily insurance, not an investment, and that is how it should be sold.

Whole life policies are enjoying a resurgence because of concern about economic uncertainty and the unrealistic interest rate assumptions used in various other policy types. Consumers like the guarantees present in whole life.

Also, whole life now has many riders that make it a lot more attractive. Such riders include survivorship life, paid up additions, and enhanced term riders.

Limited Pay Whole Life

A form of whole life where premium payments are adjusted to pay for lifetime protection but premiums stop after a specified period of time.

Interest Sensitive Whole Life

Also called Current Assumption Whole Life. In one type of ISWL, the level premium is subject to change periodically. In another, the premium remains level but may vanish. These were introduced in the 80's to reflect that decade's higher interest rates and lower mortality costs. They are non-participating, in that they do not pay dividends in the traditional sense. They guarantee that a fairly high rate of interest will be credited on the cash values, but they credit a *current* rate of interest to the policy. The money which builds up at the current interest rate is referred to as the "cash accumulation account" to distinguish it from the guaranteed cash values.

In the first type of policy, the idea is to provide a person with a whole life policy for a premium rate that is below that of traditional whole life. That will work when current interest rates are higher than the guaranteed rates. Again, the premium may fluctuate after certain periods based on how good or bad the assumptions were when the original premium was set. If the premium goes up, the policy holder can:

1. Pay it to keep the death benefit the same.
2. Pay the old lower premium and take a reduced death benefit.
3. Pay the old lower premium, keep the same death benefit, and take money out of the cash accumulation fund to make up the difference (if there is enough money in it.)

If the premium goes down:

1. Keep the death benefit and pay a lower premium.
2. Keep paying the old premium and get more death benefit.
3. Keep the old death benefit, pay the old premium, and put the difference in the cash accumulation account.

Those options relate to the type of policy that was issued to keep premiums below standard whole life rates. In the type that is designed to vanish premium, current rates of interest are credited on every dollar of policy value, so the policy owner can participate in the company's earnings from its investments.

UNIVERSAL LIFE PRODUCTS

Universal Life is right for the client who wants permanent coverage but wants the flexibility to manage the policy in terms of premiums paid, death benefits, and cash value build-up. I usually tell my clients that universal life policies place your premium dollars into three buckets. One goes to pay for mortality (the death benefit), one goes for expenses, and the other goes into an interest bearing account. The best thing about universal life is that the client has the flexibility to control his premium in order to control death benefit and cash value build-up.

When the client purchases the policy, assumptions have to be made about interest rates. These assumptions affect the level of premiums to be paid and the cash value to be built up. If interest rates fall below those used in the assumptions, not only may a client find that his cash value is not growing, he may find it used up to pay expenses and mortality costs. The only way to keep the policy in force is to increase the premiums or reduce the death benefit. Both options are available. Does this mean that universal life policies are bad? Of course not. It just means that you must be careful of your assumptions and be sure that your client does not wind up without coverage or cash value.

Variable Universal Life

This has the same features as a regular universal life policy, but allows the client to invest his cash value (the investment portion of the account) into variable accounts. These are usually managed mutual funds that invest in stocks, bonds, money market instruments, etc. The potential for greater return is available than with the traditional universal life that is dependent on interest rates for performance.

TERM INSURANCE

Term insurance is "pure" insurance for short term needs. It provides protection against financial loss resulting from death during a specified period of time. Premiums may be level or increasing during the specified period of time. Death benefit may also decrease during the time period in decreasing term policies. Increasing term is often sold as a rider to a standard term policy.

Renewable and Convertible

Most level term policies contain an option to allow the policyowner to renew the contract within certain limitations. The policy is renewable at the insured's new age with evidence of insurability. Companies usually put some limits on age, number of years, number of renewals, etc.

Level term policies and riders usually stipulate that the owner can convert all or part of the policy or rider to any form of permanent insurance without evidence of insurability. Conversion is almost always at the new age of the policyholder.

SURVIVORSHIP LIFE

Survivorship life is a traditional whole life policy that insures two lives, but the death proceeds are paid after both insureds have died. The policy has guaranteed cash values, but they are lower than similar single life policy cash values. It has fixed level premiums, and rates are lower than individual life rates because they are based on a joint life expectancy. This can minimize the impact if one of the insured has impaired health.

Riders may be available to convert to two individual policies.

This type of policy is used for:

1. Insuring key employees if a company's continued success depends on two employees, i.e., if the company could survive one death, but not both.
2. Funding a buy-sell for a business where the husband and wife are co-owners. At the death of the first spouse, the business is transferred to the surviving spouse. At the death of the second, the death benefit is used by the remaining employees to purchase the business from the estate.
3. Increasing the value of a couple's estate that they wish to pass to heirs.
4. To provide liquidity to pay estate taxes and administration costs.

DISABILITY INSURANCE

Disability insurance pays a monthly income to a person if he or she is unable to work because of injury or illness.

Disability protects a valuable asset, the ability to earn a living. When a person is disabled, her family's needs continue as well as her own. In fact, disability increases the need for income. At age 42, you are four times more likely to become disabled for at least three months before retirement than you are to die.

In any disability insurance policy, look for the following features:

1. *Definition of Disability.* Look for "own occ" coverage. This means that you will receive benefits if you cannot work in your *own occupation*, even if you work in another closely related occupation. The least desirable definition is "any occ." This means that if you can get a job (any job) you won't receive benefits. Most policies compromise between the two definitions by two methods:

a. They pay benefits under *own occ* rules for a limited period of time, such as one to five years, after which *any occ* rules take over.

b. They pay benefits if you cannot work in a "related occupation." For example, a practicing attorney might be able to teach law. If he does, he will lose benefits. If he can get work only as a ditch digger, he will not lose benefits.

Own occ features cost 5 to 15 percent more. Don't discard a policy just because it does not contain the most favorable definition of own occ. Sometimes, it makes more sense to buy higher monthly benefits than to get protection from own occ.

2. *Elimination Period.* This is the period of time you have to wait for benefits to begin after you become disabled. Perhaps it should be called the waiting period. Selecting the elimination period is usually up to the policy owner. If the client can afford a 90-day wait, then that is probably what should be brought. Thirty-day elimination periods will cost about 40 percent more than 90-day periods. Going to 180 days would save only about 15 percent of the cost of a 90-day wait.

3. *Benefit period.* Most benefits stop at age 65 when Social Security steps in. For younger clients, you may want to recommend lifetime benefits, since they may not be able to build up retirement benefits if disabled while young. This will cost about 20 percent more.

4. *Residual Benefits/Partial Disability.* With this provision, you can return to work part-time and still receive a portion of the total disability payment. These are called *residual benefits*, which continue as long as you need them. Generally, the loss of income after you return part-time must be at least 20 to 25 percent.

Partial benefits (usually 50 percent of your total benefits) are paid if you are only partially disabled. These partial benefits usually stop after three to six months.

Earned income is usually all that is covered. Check to see whether the policy covers bonuses and commissions as well. See how the income level is calculated. Many contracts use the higher of the prior 12 months or two consecutive years in the past five.

Check to see whether the insured has to be under a physician's care.

Good residual benefits will boost the premium by 20 to 25 percent.

5. *COLA.* A cost of living adjustment (COLA) will increase your monthly benefits automatically to counter inflation, usually based on the consumer price index or at a specified rate up to a specified annual maximum. This benefit costs about 25 percent more.

6. *Renewability.* Insist on a policy that is at least guaranteed renewable, which means that the insurer cannot cancel your coverage as long as you pay your premiums or raise your premium unless it boosts premiums in general.

Best is a *noncancelable* policy, which guarantees that your policy cannot be revoked and that your premium cannot be increased. This feature may cost a lot more, however.

7. *Waiver of Premium.* Why buy disability insurance if you're going to use the proceeds to pay for disability coverage? After the insured has been totally or partially disabled (usually for 90 days) the insurer "waives" additional premium payments until the policyholder's disability terminates.

8. *Maximum Benefits.* Some policies replace about 85 percent of gross income. However, you can buy policies for lower percentages. The most common are about 65 to 70 percent. The maximum benefits obtainable may depend on whether your client will take a physical before the policy is issued. If he does, he can increase the maximum from $3,000 to 4,000 per month to about $15,000 to $20,000 if that much coverage is needed.

9. *Definition of Illness and Exclusions/Limitations.* The key factor relates to when the illness or injury occurs versus when the policy begins. Generally, the illness must occur or become known *after* the policy is in force. "First manifest" means "first becomes known." Watch for the term "first contracted" or "begins." Coverage could be denied under these definitions if the illness was in existence before the policy begins *even though its existence was not known.*

MARKETING DISABILITY INSURANCE

Use the definitions in the preceding section of this chapter to explain in simple terms what a disability policy does and what it covers. Use statistics, such as those shown here, to identify clients' needs.

Current Age	Chance of Disability	Years
30	50%	4.7
40	45%	5.5
45	40%	5.8
50	34%	6.2

Of every 1,000 Americans, the number who will be disabled for at least 90 days before age 65 is listed in the following table.

Age	Number Disabled
25	522; 1 of 2 or 52%
35	480; 4 of 9 or 48%
45	401; 2 of 5 or 40%
55	266; 1 of 4 or 26%

Of all mortgage foreclosures, 3 percent are caused by death, but 48 percent are caused by disability.

Clients insure their lives, homes, cars, and other possessions, but often fail to insure their most valuable asset, their ability to earn a living. In any given year, however:

1 in 106	people die.
1 in 88	homes catch fire.
1 in 70	autos are involved in an accident resulting in disability, injury, or death.
1 in 8 people	are disabled for at least 8 days.

LONG-TERM CARE PRODUCTS

Many CPA-financial planners have a very negative view when it comes to long-term care products. They see them as health insurance. I think of them as a cross between disability and health insurance, with the greater emphasis on disability. When long-term care products were first introduced, they were fairly poor. The insurance companies simply had no history on how to write the product nor any statistics on which to base claims experience or premiums. To protect themselves, they installed "gatekeepers" in most of the early products, which kept the policies from offering good coverage.

Today's policies are much better. They offer protection for what is one of the biggest threats to savings of elderly people. The long-term care problem is a national crisis. As a financial planner, you need to include a recommendation for protection for your clients in almost every plan you prepare.

Having had my mother enter a nursing home almost three years ago, and dealing with home health care for several years prior to that, I have had firsthand experience with this major problem. I have also helped many clients to deal with it.

Unfortunately, there is no simple answer. There are the various solutions to the problem, but I have found none to be perfect, no one solution that fits every situation. I have found no way to tell you which benefits to choose if long-term care insurance is selected as the best solution for a client. However, using the information given here should give you enough information to help your client to make the best decision.

Features to Look for in Long-Term Care Products

1. *Nursing home daily benefits.* Take the average daily cost of nursing homes that your client is likely to use and convert it to a monthly cost. Subtract the client's Social Security income. That will give you the amount that the client will have to spend out of his or her own pocket per month. Convert this to a daily rate and add about 5 percent, because the client

will be able to keep a small portion of Social Security benefits. That should give you a daily rate to aim for in selecting the daily benefit in a policy.

In addition, find out whether there is a maximum amount of benefits that will be paid.

2. *Level of care.* Be sure that all levels of care are covered. Most care is at the custodial level. A policy should cover skilled nursing care, intermediate care, and custodial/personal care.

3. *Home health care.* Your client's policy should cover home health care. Staying at home as long as possible, with visiting nurses and other services, is preferable to most people. Don't be put in the position of having to tell your client that he or she will have to enter a nursing home to be covered.

4. *Length of benefits.* Find out how long benefits for each level of care will last: home health care, custodial, skilled nursing, intermediate. In most policies, you and your client can select time periods from two years to lifetime. There is no one answer for every client because of differences in age, affordability of premiums, availability of other assets, and so on.

Forty percent of patients stay in a nursing home 2-1/2 years. Only 10 percent stay more than five years. My mother has been a patient for 1-1/2 years, but had home health care for 3 years prior to that.

Many of my clients use 3 years as the period of coverage. This gives them an opportunity to give away their assets when they start to need care, and to get past the 36-month waiting period. During the 36 months, the insurance is paying. After the waiting period is over, the client may be able to qualify for Medicaid. However, watch out for income that cannot be controlled when using this option, because it may disqualify your client for Medicaid coverage. New tax legislation effective for 1994 makes it much more difficult to qualify for Medicaid in most states.

5. *Inflation adjustment.* For younger clients, I usually recommend this protection. For older people, I usually opt for a larger daily benefit. Look at the difference in cost and make your selection accordingly. Pay attention to how much the benefits go up and what the increase is based on.

6. *Elimination period.* This is the waiting period before a policy starts paying benefits. Most recommend a short waiting period of 30 days or less. Most policies have elimination periods that start with 0, 20, and go up to 100 days. Fifty percent of people who enter nursing homes stay 90 days or less. I usually differ from most experts on this point. I usually sell long-term care to prevent a person's entire estate from being consumed by illness in the last years of life. Therefore, I am very comfortable with 100-day elimination periods, even in the face of the statistics. There is also the issue of affordability and client resistance to paying premiums. If a client is reluctant to pay premiums, but can pay for 100 days of nursing home care, I think the 100-day elimination period may be preferable.

7. *Preexisting conditions.* Find out whether your client will be covered for a preexisting condition. If so, how long before coverage begins?

8. *Excluded impairments.* Ask about excluded illnesses or impairments, such as Alzheimer's disease, senility, or dementia. These should be covered.

9. *Gatekeepers.* Watch for special conditions that must be met before coverage begins. Older policies required a three-day hospital stay before an insured person could enter a nursing home. Most patients go directly from home to a nursing home.

Be sure that the policy pays if the owner can't perform the activities of daily living without assistance (eating, taking medicine, bathing, and so forth).

10. *Waiver of premium.* The premium should be waived when benefits begin. Find out what this costs.

The NAIC (National Association of Insurance Commissioners) produces a brochure for policy comparisons. You can obtain a copy by writing to the Association at 120 W. 12th Street, Suite 1100, Kansas City, MO 64105.

PART III

Attitude

TABLE OF CONTENTS

17

Awareness

Why is attitude discussed in a book about CPAs and financial planning? Because I have found that CPAs become successful in financial planning only *after* they have *decided* to become successful. They know why they want to be successful, and they know just how successful they want to be in terms of written goals. Some CPAs whom I interviewed or trained couldn't identify the reason for their success, but further questioning invariably led to their decision to become successful and to formulate written goals.

If you think that the attitudinal skills discussed in this book will be those resulting from the "feel good" type of training you may have had before, you are only partially right. Properly applied, these ideas work even for CPAs. As a group, however, we continue to earn the stereotype that others have placed upon us. We are no longer seen as bookkeepers with granny glasses and eyeshades, but we continue to be perceived as stodgy and conservative. We want to retain the conservative image that contributes to our clients' trust, but we must also cultivate the image of professionals who are capable of making creative and bold decisions that have a major impact on our clients' lives.

Before you can change a behavior pattern in order to enhance your success, you must decide to change. And to make that decision, you must be aware of the reasons for the change and believe in them. Attitudinal training delivers that awareness.

I became interested in this type of training because I felt a strong need to bring balance to my life. I found that if I spent too much time at work, I resented it and was unhappy at home and work. If I took time off for family and leisure, then I could not be happy because I felt that my business and clients were suffering. My creativity and productivity seemed to be characterized by peaks and valleys. I wanted to be happier and more productive without damaging my family, my health, my business, or my clients. I began reading books on positive thinking, attending a few seminars and listening to tapes. These all left me feeling great until I got back to the office and looked at the phone messages and my in-box.

I almost resigned myself to the fact that I was not meant to be influenced by these motivational resources. Perhaps their producers were just interested in selling tapes or charging fees. Even more comforting was the rationale that perhaps I was just too "intelligent" or perceptive to be deceived by anyone or to trick myself into being happy when things weren't really good.

After several years of haphazard dabbling in motivational training, the reason for my failure dawned on me. I didn't believe strongly enough to make the sacrifices necessary to truly apply the principles I had absorbed. I was too caught up in the day-to-day activities of running a business, community activities, and the routines of living that I could not stop to determine where I was going. In other words, I had been in a comfort zone so long that it had become a deep rut I could not seem to get out of.

I wish I could point to a momentous event or action that caused me to get out of the rut and start to apply the principles in this book. There was none. Instead, it was a *process*. To begin the process, you must learn to take advantage of your most creative and energetic periods. During one of these periods, stop the work you are doing, find a quiet place, and write down your goals and your ideas for accomplishing them. You must learn that *one hour of planning your work and your life is worth eight hours of doing productive work*. Planning saves time, it doesn't cost time. As a CPA used to billable time, remember who your most important client is. It's you. Don't worry if the ideas and plans don't flow instantly. You're not wasting time; you are thinking and you should allow yourself time to think.

In addition to expecting a book, a seminar, or a tape to be the key that I had been searching for, I also expected not to lapse. I used to think that I was subject to bouts of depression. When I read more about depression, I learned that this was not my problem. I now call my prior condition "recession." I would often experience periods of self-doubt, thinking that no matter how hard I tried, I couldn't reach the pinnacle I had been striving for. I could simply not balance all areas of my life. However, such times are fewer now, and I don't take them very seriously. They are temporary and will pass. I know where I am going and I know that circumstances, people, and events will help me on the journey.

To protect myself during these lapses, I recall Winston Churchill's famous words in a 1941 address at Harrow School, "Never give in, never give in, never, never, never, never . . . except to convictions of honor and good sense." Calvin Coolidge's famous quotation is helpful too.

- Nothing in the world takes the place of persistence.
- Talent will not; nothing is more common than unsuccessful men with talent.
- Genius will not, unrewarded genius is almost a proverb.
- Education will not, the world is full of educated derelicts.
- Determination and persistence alone are omnipotent.
- The key to success has been and will always be "press on."

The first step in any change, of course, is awareness that all is not as well as it could be. Starting from this point, the next few chapters elaborate on the following guidelines toward developing a positive attitude—and professional success:

1. Decide what you believe in.
2. List your goals in accordance with your beliefs.
3. Review your goals daily.
4. Read one hour per day.

5. Set aside at least one hour a week for "quiet time"—thinking and planning.
6. Keep lists:
   - To do
   - Goals
   - Victories
   - Wants and needs
   - Long-term projects
   - Dreams
7. Stop procrastinating.
8. Learn to harness the power of your subconscious mind.
9. Exercise at least 25 minutes four days a week.
10. Practice holistic financial planning for yourself and your clients.
11. Get smarter on technical issues.
12. Know your product, but keep it to yourself.

Ten Reasons for Adding Financial Planning

Before we embark on our journey to success, let's review some of the more important reasons that you should be involved in financial planning.

1. Your clients want and need the service. They have said so in dozens of surveys over a decade of time.
2. The other profit centers in public accounting are subject to possible shrinkage and higher costs. They are beleaguered by competition, automation, fee resistance, Congress, the president, the media.
3. Normal services offered by CPA firms no longer enjoy the level of prestige and professionalism they once did. The personal computer has brought tax return capability to your lesser competition and your clients. Audit failures have pointed out the weaknesses of financial statements according to GAAP and the audit process itself. Bookkeeping clients are doing their own accounting, using their own PCs.
4. Your current services coupled with financial planning and investment planning complement each other well and allow you once again to distinguish yourself from your competitors.
5. Traditional CPA services are negative in nature. Clients compare going to your firm to going to the dentist. Helping people reach their financial goals is a positive service.
6. Adding financial planning will bring a host of contacts and services to your firm that it has not enjoyed before.
7. You need the training to become a well-rounded financial profes-

sional. Otherwise, you will always be inferior to the polished product salesman in evaluating financial products.

8. Often, you are your clients' only financial advisor. You may be their only protection from an impoverished retirement or having their estates destroyed by taxes.

9. You could provide the only chance your clients' children have for a quality education.

10. Financial and investment planning is financially rewarding.

The savings rate in America is abysmal. Congress and the current administration may be making it worse. Millions of Americans need financial advice but do not have a broker or an advisor, because they feel they do not "qualify" or that the services will be too expensive. If you can make just one person's life better by learning this profession, wouldn't it be worth it?

18

The Necessity of Setting Goals

People don't plan to fail, they just fail to plan.

WHY YOU MUST SET GOALS

If you don't know where you are going, how can you possibly expect to get there? Setting goals, committing them to memory, and making plans for the steps you must take to achieve them, brings to your aid the people, circumstances, and events that lead to their achievement.

You may think that this statement suggests that mysterious forces will start working to help you to achieve your goals. The forces are not "mysterious." They come about as a result of your belief in and concentration on your goals. I have read and heard hundreds of accounts of individuals who have realized their goals through a chain of circumstances, events, and individuals that appeared as a result of concentration on their goals.

> You must have clear goals, and you must be able to articulate them clearly.
> —Norman Schwarzkopf

Summary of Why You Must Set Goals

1. Goals bring purpose to your life.
2. Goals bring focus, vision, and clarity to your plans.
3. Goals provide a correction to bring you back when you stray off course.
4. Goals help you in the decision-making process. By asking yourself the simple question, "Will it help me in achieving my goals?" you can more easily make decisions.
5. Goals save time. If you know where you are going, you can often find the shortest and fastest route to get there.
6. Goals reduce stress and save energy. With goals, you can avoid stress caused by conflicting decisions, your mind is less cluttered, and you spend less time chasing projects that are not leading toward your goals.
7. Goals contribute to happiness and inner peace. You have a vision of where you are going; what you want to accomplish, and how others will be helped by your achievement.
8. Goals help to avoid procrastination. One of the reasons for procrastination is indecision, failure to see value in what we are about to do. If a task involves your goals, you will be motivated to do it.
9. Setting goals and adjusting them to your changing needs and circumstances opens your mind to new ideas and possibilities.
10. Goals help you to become a better thinker.

HOW TO SET GOALS

If goal setting is so important, why don't more people do it? In a 1953 study at Harvard University, a survey of the graduating seniors found that only 3 percent had goals. In a follow-up 20 years later, the net worth of those constituting that 3 percent was greater than the net worth of the entire other 97 percent. Why didn't the 97 percent do something that seems so simple?

- They didn't realize the importance of goals.
- They didn't know how to set goals.
- They were reluctant to write down their goals because of the fear of failure. If they had no goals, then they didn't have to face the prospect of not meeting them.
- They feared ridicule (rejection) for not meeting their goals if others found out about them.

Although I started long ago, I am still perfecting the art of goal setting. I am still learning. You will probably develop your own style after a period of time, but the steps offered here are those that have worked for me.

Instead of just thinking of goals related to daily life and business, try thinking of your hopes, dreams, desires, and aspirations. These are the real goals we address here.

Goal Setting

1. Find a quiet place where you feel comfortable and can relax without interruption. Try to choose a time when you are in a good mood. Go through some relaxation techniques so that your thoughts can flow easily. Try to clear your mind of all conscious thoughts. Stay in the relaxed mode for approximately 15 minutes.

2. Use your computer or a notepad, whichever you prefer, and set up five sheets:

    a. Family

    b. Emotional and Spiritual

    c. Career and Financial

    d. Physical

    e. Major Definitive Purpose

3. Write the acronym SMART on the bottom line of each sheet.

  S = specific

  M = measurable

  A = achievable

  R = realistic

  T = tangible

After you have written down all your goals (don't write yet), you will make sure that each one meets the SMART test. If it does not, it should be reworded until it does. For example, under Emotional, many people write, "I want to be happy"—a great goal that everyone shares, but it fails the test. It is easy to get goals to meet the SMART test in categories c and d under item 2, but more difficult in a, b, and e. Allow yourself some leeway on the SMART test for these categories, especially on the major definitive purpose. That is hard to measure at first.

4. Start the thought process by thinking about what you want in your life in each of the areas listed. Goals should be something you really want for yourself.

5. Start writing goals randomly on the sheets as they occur to you. Don't try to write as if your goals are going to be published in the local newspaper. These are for you, and you will always be in control of who sees them. Don't put them to the SMART test until you are finished. Just let your writing and thoughts flow freely.

6. As you write, *visualize* what it will look and feel like to actually accomplish your goals. What would you do, where would you go, how would you feel, what would you say, what would you buy, what would your friends and family say? For example, if your goal is to be the top producer for next year, visualize yourself accepting an award and making a speech with your family watching.

You become what you think about—to achieve success in any area, you must have a mental picture of your idea of success

7. When you have finished writing down all the goals that come to mind, give them the SMART test and restate as needed.

8. Now subject each goal to another test. For each goal, answer these questions:

- Do I really want it? (the Want test).
- Do I need it? If you want it so much that the want won't go away, then you need it (the Need test).
- Am I willing to do what it takes to get it? Am I willing to spend time and money and experience the pain of personal growth in order to reach it? (the Sacrifice test).
- Do I have what it takes to reach it? (Refers to the realistic and achievable part of the SMART test). This step requires you to take stock of your mental and physical resources to see whether your goal is really attainable. That doesn't mean to discard goals that require you to stretch. This is a test to see whether you are committed enough to use what you have, and to go out and get more of what is needed, to achieve your goal. If you truly don't believe in the goal, then maybe it isn't a goal after all (the Resource test).

If your goals don't meet these tests, then move them to a sixth page, en-titled Dreams. You may want to change these dreams to goals later.

9. Restate the goals in present tense as if they were already accomplished. This was difficult for me to do. It somehow seemed to be misleading or deceptive. I was always taught never to pretend to be something you are not. Never fake it. I now believe it is OK and productive to "fake it till you make it."

10. Set target dates for the financial and career goals and other goals that seem suited to a target date.

11. Reread your goals and start another free-thinking session about what your *major definitive purpose* in life should be. This goal should encompass the "theme" set by the goals you have listed, taking into account your profession, your talents, abilities, and resources. Think about what you can do to help others while achieving your own goals. Why were you put here?

After you have completed the goals and your major definitive purpose, you should have a list that needs only a little cleaning up to get started toward accomplishment. The list will change frequently as you hone your goal-setting skills. If your list of goals is long, you may want to break them down even further and prioritize them as to importance. For example, I have a list of things I want to own that I consider by-products of my goals list. If your list is very long, then do prioritize it by importance and by target dates. *Make a summary list of your most important goals*. This is the list you will refer to *daily*.

This is where commitment and persistence come in. I didn't review my goals daily after I first followed the preceding guidelines. That was a mistake. Many people reduce their goals to index cards and carry them with them. Others have them memorized. Some have them on tape, which makes change and updating easy.

ESTABLISHING A BELIEF SYSTEM

Establishing a belief system or determining what my belief system is was more difficult for me than setting goals. Many trainers start with the belief system before they set goals. I think either method is acceptable. Almost everyone has a belief system; some just have difficulty in expressing it. What does a belief system have to do with setting goals? Research has shown that if your goals are not congruent with your belief system, you will either fail to achieve your goals or goal achievement will leave you asking, "Is that all there is?" For example, if one of your goals is to own a Corvette convertible, but your belief system says that indulging in such extravagance is wrong and selfish, then you will either fail to reach your goal of having a Corvette, or you will feel guilty all the time you own it.

How do you find out what your beliefs are?

1. Go back to step 1 under "Goal Setting." Find a quiet place to let your mind wander.
2. Review your goals to see what beliefs about yourself and life in general they conjure up.
3. Start writing your beliefs as they come to you. Don't try to make them perfect or grammatically correct, just write. You can polish them later.
4. It occasionally helps to separate your beliefs into the same categories as your goals (i.e., family, career and financial, etc.).

To get you started, I offer some examples of my own beliefs.

Family

I believe that having an association with a loving family is one of life's greatest pleasures and one of the most important goals to strive for. I also believe that it is possible for a person to have a successful career without damaging his or her family relationships. In fact, a successful career usually enhances such relationships.

Emotional and Spiritual

I believe that happiness is a state of mind, not a state of affairs, and that you choose to be happy. I also believe that tapping the power of the subconscious mind is harmonious with the power of prayer and my religious beliefs.

I believe that people must accept responsibility for their actions and for their reactions to things that happen to them.

I believe that I must have a sense of humor about life's ups and downs and that setbacks must not be taken so seriously. We must learn from our mistakes but not dwell on them.

Career and Financial

I believe that selfless service to others is an essential part of financial and career success. I believe that your rewards in life will be in direct proportion to the value of your service to others. I believe that you should do what you love, love what you do, and that money will take care of itself.

I believe that career and financial success are harmonious with religion, spirituality, and family.

Physical

I believe that the mind is the most powerful healing force. I believe that our bodies must be treated with respect and care in order to use them completely to meet our goals.

MONITORING GOALS WITH A MENTOR

As mentioned earlier, goals can be kept private. However, if you are comfortable with such a relationship, you might try sharing career and financial goals (as they relate to career) with a mentor or partner. Research has shown this to be very effective. It brings discipline to the process. The partner or mentor will force you to look at where you are in the goal attainment process and what steps you need to take to get on track. The mentor can also provide encouragement and direction. Without a periodic review by an outside party, most people will not have the self-discipline to keep going if they "drop the ball" for even a short period of time.

Mentoring also forces realism into the goal-setting process. If you feel that you will never be called to task for your goals, you may have a tendency to set unrealistic ones or to not set them at all. A good rule of thumb is to discuss your goals at least four hours per year with your mentor.

What should be included in the monitoring process?

1. Give a report on the status of your progress toward achieving your goals.
2. Discuss problems encountered, success stories.
3. Show a breakdown of your goals into manageable segments. For example, if your goal is to realize $100,000 in gross commissions this year, then you must earn $8,333 per month, $1,923 per week, or $385 per day. This can be further translated to $2,500,000 in sales per year, $208,333 per month, $48,080 per week, $9,616 per day, or $1,202 per hour. Find a designation that suits you and that you can commit to memory.
4. Go through the goal accomplishment process. Discuss the activities that must be performed and which ones are being done, possibly adding or deleting activities that are not working.
5. Discuss the reasons for not meeting goals. Excuses should not be allowed (typically, no time, client demands; general excuses indicating lack of good time management, focus, or simply not taking the program seriously).
6. If goals are consistently not being met, review the goal-setting process and subject your goals to the tests described earlier.

Remember—The purpose of the review is not to criticize or condemn, but to help.

STEPS TO GOAL ACHIEVEMENT

We have discussed why goals are needed, how to set them, how to make them harmonious with your belief system, and how to monitor them. We are ready to discuss the actual process of goal achievement.

Actually, the most important part of goal achievement has already been covered. These essential steps are worthy of repeating:

1. Commit your goals to writing.
2. Make sure that they are congruent with your belief system.
3. Subject your goals to the SMART test, the Want test, the Need test, the Sacrifice test, and the Resource test.
4. Decide on your major definitive purpose in life.
5. Visualize how you will look and feel when you accomplish your goals. Sense and experience the reality of your outcome as already being true. Verify that your outcome is what you really and truly want.
6. State your goals in the present tense and in positive terms: "I have $5 million of client funds under management. That money is attracting more and more referrals, and I am enjoying my new challenges and new professionalism."
7. Set target dates beside your goals where applicable. This can be confusing if you have stated the goals as if they are already taking place. I suggest keeping a separate copy for target dates.
8. Select the most important goals you have for this year. Try to limit the selection to 10.
9. Put the most important goals on cards that will be available for referral during the day. Post them in plain sight. Possibly record them in your own voice and play them daily for at least 21 days. By then you should have them committed to memory.
10. Repeat your goals aloud daily (possibly while exercising).
11. Monitor your goals with a mentor.

If you have completed these 11 essential steps and keep the process going until it becomes a habit (usually 21 days), you will start to attract the circumstances, resources, events, and people that will help you to achieve your goals.

Act boldly, and unseen forces will come to your aid.

There are two schools of thought on the rest of the steps required to accomplish your goals. One holds that these 11 steps are all that are required. The other believes that goals must be accompanied by action plans, that the "unseen forces" don't come until you do some work yourself. Being a pragmatic accountant, I think both points of view are valuable. Here are the remaining steps to ensure that no bases are left uncovered.

12. Break down your goals into manageable parts. (This may have already been done in the monitoring step.) If your goal is stated as an annual amount, I recommend breaking it down into months, weeks, days, and even hours. This will allow you to monitor progress.

13. List your most important resources for achieving your goals. For example: I am a CPA, I have 500 clients who trust me, I am personable, a good speaker, and so on.

14. List three to five times when you were successful in using your resources. For example: I built my tax practice from 20 clients to 200 in only two years.

15. Describe the kind of person you would need to become to effect the outcome you want for the goals you established. For example: I need to be confident and persuasive, motivated and upbeat.

16. Write down what prevents you from having the things you want right now. For example: Fear of failure, procrastination, fear of success (I don't deserve it).

17. List the names of people who have achieved goals similar to yours.

18. List the actions that you would need to take to achieve each goal. Put each of your goals on a separate sheet. Under the goal or beside it, make a column for actions. Visualize the goal already accomplished. Then think back to what actions you would have taken to accomplish the goal. For example, if your goal is to set up five retirement plans during the year, your action steps might be:

   • Review my client files for small businesses.

   • Pull their tax returns and determine which ones do not have plans and which do.

   • Obtain a questionnaire for small businesses that have plans and one for those that do not.

   • Send letters to at least 50 on the list.

   • Follow up with phone calls to set appointments. Use TOPS questions. Have the questions ready before calling. Set at least 10 appointments.

   • Offer to do a free evaluation and survey of employees to determine which type of plan the employer needs, what the employees want, and so on.

   • Obtain a questionnaire from a product sponsor, third-party administrator, and so forth to gather data.

   • Follow up with an appointment to present a plan with at least 10 employers.

   • Close five retirement plans.

   • Implement the plans and enroll employees.

As you can see, this list is in chronological sequence, involving all of the critical steps to a good action plan: *planning, implementation, and follow-up.*

The actual process of setting up a marketing plan using market niches, goals, and action steps is discussed in Part I of this book.

People with goals succeed because they know where they're going.
—Earl Nightingale

I do not think there is any other quality so essential to success of any kind as the quality of perseverance. It overcomes almost anything, even nature.
—John D. Rockefeller

19

Conserving Your Most
Valuable Resource—Time

Dost thou love life? Then do not squander time; for that's the stuff life is made of.

—Benjamin Franklin

All of us have the same amount of time. Some just squeeze more productivity and enjoyment out of every hour than others. This chapter is devoted to helping you to use this unique resource better. Time is a unique resource; it cannot be stockpiled or accumulated and it cannot be turned off. Time is life.

CPAs, like many other professionals, sell time. When you sell time, its value as a commodity becomes real. Our natural inclination is to think in terms of rates per hour. We set up time-keeping systems to ensure that our clients will be billed properly. In spite of time systems, I continually found that I was short on billable versus nonbillable time. I worked on getting more billable time. I separated all activities into billable versus nonbillable. But that attitude tends to get your life out of balance. One day I made the mistake of calculating what I would make if 100 percent of my working hours were billable. It wasn't enough. That's when I decided I had to find a way to get more out of time. Since most of us do keep time records out of necessity, you have probably been alerted to the difficulty of managing time.

Most CPAs stop there. They accept this as part of the price of the profession and continue to let time control their lives. If you practice following the ideas in this chapter, they will help you to control time and your life. You will start to feel better about your profession and about life in general.

WHY WE MUST MANAGE TIME

There are a great many benefits in learning to manage time wisely. Time management:

- Is profitable. Time is life, but it is also money. Managing time is financially rewarding.
- Reduces stress. If you often have that "out of control" feeling, then you are leading a life that is too stressful.
- Is essential to high self-esteem and a balanced, happy life.

There are two misconceptions that work against us in learning to become excellent time managers.

1. *Organized people are boring.* We've all heard such phrases as "Time management stifles my creativity," "I just want to go with the flow," "Don't take away my spontaneity."

That's the backward way to look at time management. Taking control of time actually stimulates creativity and allows your spirit and thoughts to soar. Managing time allows us to be more productive while still having time for family and leisure activities. It also allows time to think.

It's the people who don't manage time who suffer. They often lead unbalanced, nonproductive lives. They may be free spirits, but they are usually plagued with self-doubt, low productivity, and low self-esteem. Their lives are a series of extreme highs and lows—or a continuous low. A person who controls his or her time and life can avoid many of the extreme fluctuations.

2. *Rushing, always talking on the phone, being late to appointments, and inability to attend meetings owing to "time constraints" are often seen as signs of a prosperous, busy, productive person.* Just the opposite is true. These are characteristics of people who are not in control of their time. Time is controlling them. Time managers are calm, relaxed, able to focus on the task at hand without taking phone calls or interruptions, show up at meetings on time, and attend educational seminars from start to finish.

I was a "closet" time manager for many years. I even felt guilty for not joining the mad dash to the telephone at every break in a conference. I felt deprived by not talking on a portable phone during seminars. I felt lonely arriving at meetings on time. Maybe I just wasn't as busy as all these other people who seemed to take such pride in their busyness. But watching people whom I knew to be successful brought me out of the closet. The message? Take pride in time management.

> When you are organized, you have a special power
> You walk with a sure sense of purpose.
> Your priorities are clear in your mind
> You orchestrate complex events with a masterful touch
> Things fall into place when you reveal your plans
> You move smoothly from one project to the next with no wasted motion
> Throughout the day, you gain stamina and momentum as your successes build.
> People believe your promises because you always follow through
> When you enter a meeting, you're prepared for whatever they throw at you
> When at last you show your hand, you're a winner
> —Mark McCormack, Author of *What They Don't Teach You at Harvard Business School*

HOW TO GET CONTROL OF TIME

There are certain definite steps to getting control of time, which are discussed in the following paragraphs.

1. *Decide* that time management is important to your health, wellbeing, and prosperity. This is essential to the implementation of the rec-

ommended steps in the rest of this program. If you are not convinced, review the reasons given earlier.

2. *Set goals.* For the very reasons that goals are important generally, they are also essential in time management.

3. *Make and keep lists.* These lists can be useful in getting control of your time:

A. Daily to-do lists.

B. To-do lists for tomorrow and for the next 30 days.

C. Goals (separated into the five major categories).

D. Specific project and long-term lists (such as a tax season marketing program or another specific marketing segment big enough to have its own list).

E. Dreams.

F. Things I want to own.

G. Places I want to go.

H. Victory list (goals I have met, significant projects completed, dreams come true, things I now own that I wanted, places I have been).

You might look at lists A, B, and C every day; D at least once a week; E once a month; F when you feel like it or when you add to it; G when you see or read something that makes you want to go somewhere; H when you are updating any other list and see something that is now complete. It's a satisfying feeling to view the victory list. These lists work just like any other goal list. Events, circumstances, and people will come to you to help you attain the item you want if it is a true "want" that stays long enough to qualify as a "need." See the sample list in Form 19.1.

Daily To-Do Lists

If you don't keep daily to-do lists, you don't like prosperity and serenity. You like havoc, chaos, long hours, and low productivity. You may be doing all right without these lists, but you will do immeasurably better with them.

Some people say they don't have time to make lists. You don't have time *not* to make lists. Lists don't cost time, they provide you with direction for daily activities. Why should you make to-do lists every day, and when should you do them?

- Preferably, you should make a to-do list before you go home each day. Some people like to wake early in the morning and make a list. Either is effective. Making a list at the end of the day will activate your subconscious to work on the next day's activities during the night. Making it in the middle of the day is the worst time, but it is still better than nothing. At least the last half of the day will be productive.

Form 19.1   Sample To-Do List

Date: _____   Name: _____
To-Do List For:
Today _____   Tomorrow _____   Short-Term _____
Long-Term _____

Item #	Project	*	$	Tot. Pts.	Prior-ities	Com-plete
1	REVIEW GOALS	***				
2	PREPARE TO-DO LIST	***				
3						
4						
5						
6						
7						
8						
9						
10						
11						
12						

* Urgency Rating one to three stars—10 points each.
$ Value Rating one to three dollar signs—20 points each.

- To-do lists take the clutter out of your mind. Without lists, you will constantly be putting out fires or doing nothing because you can't think of what it was you were supposed to do.
- You won't forget as many things.
- You will be able to prioritize your tasks and focus better on what is important. I prioritize based on two factors:
  1. Value in terms of dollars.
  2. Urgency (the degree of pain that will occur if the job is not done today).

- Adding to the list on a daily basis when a new task comes up keeps you focused on the task at hand, rather than letting your mind wander to the project that can wait.
- Crossing things off the list gives you a great feeling of accomplishment.

If you find that you keep writing and rewriting the same list, this means that you are not using your list during the day or you are not being honest when you make it out. Do you need to do the things on the list or not? If you do, then do them. If not, don't put them on the list.

What about tasks that arise that you can't possibly do today or tomorrow? I keep a page for each day for at least 30 days out. When a new task comes up, I just select a day when I think I can tackle it and write it down on that day's list. It is bound to come up before it causes me grief for not having it done. This type of task is different from the long-term project discussed next.

Project and Long-Term Lists

Keeping long-term and project lists separate from daily to-dos can be confusing. There is bound to be a point when the two overlap. Most computer programs allow specific project lists to "merge" into your daily to-dos. That is ideal. If you are keeping the lists by hand or your software doesn't do the merging, then you have to look at your project lists often or manually list the tasks on your project list on your daily to-do list.

What do I mean by a project list and a long-term list? Why bother to have them if you are going to merge them with the daily to-do lists anyway? Project lists are specific larger projects that require the completion of several tasks. Often, these tasks must be completed in sequential order. *Each task on the list must be assigned a due date.* Moreover, the project may involve several people and separate meetings. If the tasks are commingled with your daily to-dos, then it is hard to determine the total status of the project.

How does a project list differ from a long-term list? Long-term lists usually contain projects as well as tasks that have not been assigned due dates as yet. They are things you want to do and possibly need to do. However, you may not yet have the resources to do them, or the timing may not be right to do them now. So why keep a long-term list? Because that is part of planning. The long-term list is part of your overall plan and contains projects and tasks that you don't want to forget. That's what lists are all about—not forgetting.

The Importance of Lists

You have to make only one list each day—the daily to-do list. You look at your goal list every day, but it is only redone when you feel the need (usually every 60 days or so). You will probably need to review your project list at least twice a week, depending on the urgency and importance of the project, the people who are assisting you, and so forth. Also, remember the alternative—chaos and stress.

If you are working by yourself or with only a limited staff, all the more reason for keeping lists. In a big corporation, mistakes, missed deadlines, and unhappy customers are commonplace; they can go on for a long time. You, however, can't afford them for even a short time.

To summarize:

1. Keep a daily to-do list. Prioritize each project according to dollar value and urgency.
2. Keep separate sheets set up for 30 days ahead if you are using a manual system.
3. Keep project lists for major projects. List the tasks to be done for a project in priority order (may have to be sequential).
4. Be sure that the tasks on your project lists are always included on your daily to-do lists as they come due.
5. Maintain long-term lists to keep from forgetting projects or tasks that do not have due dates yet.
6. Review your goals daily.
7. Review your Dreams, Wants, and Needs lists as the thoughts enter your mind, to add to them or think about them.
8. Revise your Goals list every 60 days or so.
9. As you revise your Goals list, add to your Victories list.

Memorize these nine steps. Practice the procedure for at least 21 days. By the end of that time, it will become habit.

20

Managing Time and People

Many CPAs are partners in a small firm or are sole proprietors. Not only must they manage their own time, but other people's time as well. Some employees may be concerned about time only in the context of what they will be paid per hour, time off, and quitting time. It is up to you to set a good example. This chapter shows you how to do that. First, a caution: don't expect perfection in getting other people to be as concerned as you are about making your business profitable. I admit to suffering a good deal of frustration in this area because I expected too much too soon. Building a good team is essential to your success, but it is a long process that requires commitment. Your goals should be to:

1. Set a good example.
2. Provide the tools and skills necessary for your employees to be efficient.
3. Monitor their progress.
4. Provide guidance, direction, and motivation.
5. Delegate to your staff and give them responsibility.

The following paragraphs offer guidelines to meeting these goals:

All Staff members should maintain daily to-do lists. They should use them for *personal* as well as *work* tasks. They can even write down things such as "Run before breakfast," "Attend Rotary Club." Writing these things down and marking them off as accomplishments keeps the juices flowing.

Purchase a task or project management software system. This system should be operated by someone other than yourself. Otherwise, you will be relegated to the role of monitor and bookkeeper and will probably be overwhelmed by your own system.

Task lists for every staff member must be input into a central system. Personal tasks are an exception. We use a small form called a task assignment sheet that is routed to the central person. Whether you use a manual system or software, it should be "automatic" that tasks are fed into a central system at the same time that they are added to individual to-do lists. All tasks must be given a due date. Most systems allow you to enter the assignee and the supervisor. Each week, the employee in charge of the central monitoring system will print:

1. A consolidated list of everything that was due the prior week and what is coming due the next week.
2. A list of each employee's tasks in order of due date.
3. A list of all projects with tasks.

Weekly staff meetings must be held to report on all tasks and projects. Lists should be printed and distributed at least 24 hours prior to the scheduled weekly staff meeting. All staff members should compare the central list to their own to make sure they are ready to report during the staff meeting. At the meeting, each project for the past week and the next week is read and reported on by the responsible party. Each project must be announced as complete, changed, eliminated for a reason, or moved to a new date with reason given.

Each staff meeting should have an agenda. This is a typical one:

1. Read aloud projects and reports.
2. Special report by each staff member.
3. New products.
4. Problems incurred with clients or software, new tax laws, or other circumstances.
5. New employees, announcements about existing staff, and other personnel matters.

The meeting should last no longer than an hour; many will be over in less than half that time.

Meetings are notorious time wasters. However, a regularly scheduled meeting like this will keep communication flowing throughout the firm, motivate the completion of projects, monitor progress on special projects, and eliminate the necessity of so many special meetings that interrupt everyone's schedule. They also provide a forum for you to give instructions without embarrassment to specific individuals, and for employees to offer recommendations and show their value. We found that tax season meetings were especially valuable. We could discuss returns that had problems so that everyone knew what was going on when a client called in about his or her return (all tax returns are assigned a project automatically when the client's file is pulled).

What about recurring tasks? We keep a list called the End of Month List. It is a check-off sheet that must be completed by month end. If projects remain incomplete at month end, they are added to the master task list. The End of Month list is a list of all reports that must be done during the month, regularly scheduled payments that must be made, and so forth. If you have a software system, I suggest that you use the recurring task feature to add these to your system like any other tasks. A good system will feed your recurring task into the system and pop up reminders for you when the task is due.

Chapter 2 of this book discusses how to develop a marketing plan. The marketing plan should be handled as a combination recurring task list (because many of the tasks are recurring) and a major project list (because many of the tasks for each marketing category must be performed in a sequential manner).

DELEGATE TO YOUR STAFF

I only do what only I can do.

—Jim Ainsworth

Many sole proprietors have either no employees or only one. That is the way I started out. However, as soon as I got enough billings to keep myself busy, I added staff as quickly as I could. You should always pay someone at a lower rate while you do something at a higher rate.

Why have a staff if you don't delegate to them? Like a lot of entrepreneurs, I was a "control freak" for many years. Nobody could do the job as well as I could: "If I want it done well, I had better do it myself." I soon realized that with that attitude, staff became a liability rather than an asset.

Numerous studies have shown that the primary source of motivation for people is a sense of accomplishment and importance and recognition for a job well done. The only way to get a sense of importance and accomplishment is to have responsibility. Many CPA businesses are too small to offer vertical growth for employees. To keep a good employee, you must offer growth through expansion of responsibilities, which leads to new opportunities. Here are some ideas for delegating:

1. Carefully screen people before you hire them. You may make a few mistakes, but not as many as when you hire in a panic.
2. Don't concentrate heavily on particular skills (although they are important). Instead, concentrate on attitude, enthusiasm, and general intelligence.
3. Give your employees slightly more responsibility than they think they can handle.
4. Try to stay out of the details while they are doing the job.
5. Input the job into your monitoring system and require reports during staff meetings.
6. Don't let staff reverse-delegate the job back to you little by little. Reverse delegation is a serious problem. It is human nature for people to take the path of least resistance and to avoid getting out of their comfort zone. You should always keep your staff slightly out of their comfort zone.

To prevent them from giving a project back to you piece by piece, just refuse to accept it.

The watchwords in my office are *think, follow through, and finish*. These concepts can be helpful in managing your own time and that of others.

Think. To my associates, this means that I want them to think about what they have just done or asked me about. The correct way to do it or the answer to the question is clearly within their abilities. It also means that I want them to give me a recommended solution as if they were the owners of the business.

Follow through means just what it says. Don't let a project just hang there. It is usually used in the context of a project that has no specific deadline for completion because a series of sequential events have to occur before the project is brought to a conclusion. I found that such projects tended to get stopped in the middle, because staff would get a sense of completion from doing several steps. They also had a problem with time sequence. If a project did not have a deadline for completion, then they tended to drop the ball. There is a natural resistance to such projects because of the knowledge that one event must end before the next one begins. Sales or marketing projects that require the customer to take some form of action before the next step can occur are typical of this type of resistance. To avoid this, you must handle these as projects with tasks in your system. Assign deadlines to all tasks even though they are sequential.

Finish. You need to keep employees from taking a project to the edge of their comfort zone, then giving it back to you to finish. In many cases, you would spend less time if you had started the project and carried it through to completion rather than picking it up in the middle. You must demand that your employees finish the projects you assign them.

> Character is the ability to follow through on a task after the enthusiasm has waned.

Many of the steps I have outlined will not work the first or even the second time. You must be persistent and continuous in your efforts if you are going to build a great team. Here is a summary of tasks for managing time when other people are involved:

1. Employees must maintain daily to-do lists.
2. Enter all tasks of all employees into a central system maintained by someone other than yourself.
3. Print a consolidated list and separate lists for each employee prior to your weekly staff meeting. Separate lists of tasks by major project.
4. Report on all projects during the weekly meeting.
5. Follow a stated agenda for the rest of the reports for the staff meeting.
6. Be sure that all recurring tasks are included in your central system.
7. Delegate; use the terms *think*, *follow through*, and *finish*.

You now have a system for monitoring your own projects as well as those of your staff. Nothing should "drop through the cracks" in this system. Clients should have their projects done on time, all billable time should be captured, and your stress should be reduced.

THE THIEVES OF TIME

Thief 1—Procrastination

Most of us are natural procrastinators. We have a tendency to take the path of least resistance, the one that leads downhill. Consider these ways to get this most terrible of thieves out of your life.

1. *Get rid of all the myths about procrastination.* People love to brag about being procrastinators. It is socially acceptable. We believe that it makes us more loved and accepted by our friends and peers. To say in a group that you never procrastinate is like saying, ''I am smarter than everyone here.'' You don't have to boast of being self-disciplined, but you will be admired for it even if people don't want to admit it.

Procrastination is a detriment to your personal and professional life. It affects you and everyone around you negatively. It is not easy to get rid of, but you can overcome this tendency if you really want to.

2. *Decide that you want to stop being a procrastinator.*

3. *Start keeping track of instances of your procrastination.* List what negative effect procrastination had in each case. List what positive effects may have occurred if you had not procrastinated.

4. *Stop rationalizing and making excuses for putting things off.*

5. *Use the time management techniques outlined in this book.*

Need some helpful hints to use every day? Here they are:

Practice Identifying Saddle Burrs. Learn to distinguish between what is *significant* versus what is *urgent*. This was the most important step for me in overcoming procrastination. However, it is also one of these things that are profoundly simple in concept but exceedingly difficult to explain or implement.

Most time management courses and books concentrate on the priority approach and the A, B, C rating of projects. This is valid, but they also usually tell you to rate projects in terms of their *positive* benefits. Many go a step further and tell you to rate projects as to the *negative* things that will happen if they are not done. In practice, however, most of us still have difficulty in properly prioritizing projects because we overlook the projects that *seem* to be insignificant. Many of these projects are mundane, routine tasks that appear to have little or no positive benefit. We just naturally move them down the priority scale. *That is the most common mistake in time management.*

I call these little projects saddle burrs. Think of a burr under the saddle of a horse you are riding. The horse is your business or a client. The burr is a small inconvenience at first, but it gradually grows into a major pain for the horse and he will throw you from the saddle because of it. Think of the pain from being thrown and how you could have avoided it by simply looking under the saddle and removing the burr.

Saddle burrs must be removed instantly. They are urgent tasks that will cause you much grief if they are not done right away. You can spot saddle burrs by evaluating the negative consequences of not doing important tasks. Here are some examples of saddle burrs:

a. Invoices that are due for payment. OK, you rationalize, its tax season and your supplier understands. I have a policy that all bills will be paid within 48 hours after they arrive. The only exceptions are those that are in dispute and those that cannot be confirmed as to receipt of services or products. What happens if you don't pay bills right away?

   • You think you have more spendable cash than you really do.
   • Either your monthly financial statements are off, or you have to spend a lot of time accruing unpaid invoices. Accruing them usually adds 400 percent to their handling time.

     Remember, you have to reverse the accrual or make sure that all invoices are coded against accounts payable. Don't bother with accruing? OK—then your cash and your financials are wrong.
   • Your suppliers think you are a poor manager of time and business and spread the word among your clients.
   • You forget why you bought the service or product or what you did with it when you got it. This adds 200 percent to handling time.
   • It's much harder to challenge a questionable invoice after you have let the invoice become delinquent or waited until the last minute to pay.
   • You miss discounts.

b. Not preparing financial statements monthly. I know that I should not have to tell CPAs to prepare financial statements monthly, but I also know that many do not. Your own statements must be given priority over those of your clients.

   • You cannot effectively manage a business without having current financial statements.
   • Sooner or later, you will be embarrassed by a client, a banker, or a creditor when you, a CPA, cannot produce current financial statements for your own business at a moment's notice.
   • It takes approximately twice as long to produce financial state-

ments after the information has gone stale than when the information is current.

c. Not returning telephone calls within 24 hours. The telephone as another thief of time is discussed later, but this concerns returning telephone calls only.

- If you do not return calls within 24 hours, you make your caller's life miserable and he or she will return the favor.
- You are not perceived as the busy executive, but as a harried, unorganized person whom your caller won't recommend to others because you can't manage your own affairs.
- You will miss opportunities.
- If urgent action is required as a result of the phone call, you may miss the deadline.
- Your caller may be available for only a short period of time.

There are exceptions to this rule. Some calls can be delayed for longer than 24 hours, and some should never be returned. Don't misunderstand me to say that you should *take* all calls; rather, you should *return* all calls within 24 hours—it's a matter of courtesy.

Here are some other examples of saddle burrs. You can fill in the negative consequences.

d. Not making your daily to-do list.
e. Not having weekly staff meetings.
f. Not writing down your goals or updating them.
g. Not exercising.
h. Not preparing project lists in time-line order before starting on a major project.
i. Not preparing small financial plans, just delving right into product presentations.
j. Not doing your daily reading.
k. Not putting "think breaks" on your calendar.

Are you starting to see the similarity of the saddle burrs? They usually have these common traits:

- They can be remedied quickly, but if not remedied, no immediate pain results.
- Their negative effects can be long-term and severe.
- They usually involve poor habit patterns.
- They involve path-of-least-resistance thinking: Not doing them now

won't hurt me this instant, and they won't have an immediate positive impact either.

- Taking care of saddle burrs indicates habit patterns, rather than short-term conscious action.
- Long-term effects of ignoring them are severe.
- Taking care of them later rather than now increases the time required exponentially—usually 500 percent!

Learn the Elephant and Pie Approach. How do you eat an elephant? One bite at a time. That's how you tackle big or unpleasant projects. Since I would rather eat pies than elephants, I visualize each major project as a big pie with several slices. Some slices are invariably easier to "eat" than others. I usually start with one of those. The key is to *get started*!

Remember the 500 Percent Rule. When you throw a project into a corner, the time required to complete it starts growing exponentially, usually expanding to 500 percent of what it would have taken to do it when the project was fresh. This is because of a phenomenon of the mind that I cannot explain. I have tested it, however, and the 500 percent rule almost always works. I really started to believe it when I noticed it was true for easy projects as well as long and difficult ones. Somehow, a project loses its appeal and value as it gets older. It starts to grow in your mind and makes you feel guilty. The solution is to do it on time and save the 500 percent!

Develop a Speed Mentality. The speed mentality simply recognizes that tasks must be performed as rapidly as possible to promote efficiency and profitability. It doesn't mean that your heart rate is pumping to maximum capacity. Once you recognize that speed is important, you can relax and operate with efficiency. If you do not have a speed mentality, you will endure greater stress when a job must be done quickly, because you must change your normal work habits to get it done.

Visualize Completing the Project. Instead of seeing yourself going through the drudgery of doing the project and encountering all the difficulties, visualize yourself reaping the rewards of a completed job.

Plan Rewards for Yourself. As each project is completed, give yourself a small reward. Rewards can range from something as simple as having a Coke break, playing a round of golf, or taking a cruise. The only rules are that the reward should be decided in advance and should reflect the value of the completed task or portion thereof. Have you ever noticed how much more productive you are just before a vacation? The concept works!

Be Decisive. Analyze your actions to see whether you are allowing any projects to be delayed because you can't make a decision. Are you waiting until this or that takes place, or this particular other project is complete, or your child gets out of school, or tax season is over, or this audit is completed? Ask yourself these questions:

- Does the project involve something that leads me toward my goals?
- Is it going to make me feel good when it is finished?

If the answer is yes, do it now!

Learn to Focus. One of the most important qualities that distinguishes winners from losers is the ability to adopt a long-term perspective. Many highly intelligent, competent people are unable to focus on a particular project and carry it through to completion. They are continually distracted by other projects, people, mail, and so forth. They have a speed mentality, work fast, and generally get a lot of small things done, but are unable to complete the big projects. They also have difficulty with the urgent tasks that may appear insignificant (saddle burrs). Thus, they live their lives "behind the eight ball." They are excellent candidates for the problems that come with uncontrolled stress.

How do you learn to focus, follow through, and finish?

a. Set goals and read them daily.
b. Admit your problem. (Denial of the existence of this problem is prevalent because the individuals see themselves as high achievers and intelligent.)
c. Follow the rules of good time management. This is doubly important if you have this problem. You must organize each day around your task list.
d. Designate blocked-off portions of time on your calendar to work on big projects. Keep the appointment with yourself and the project.
e. Time alone for thinking is essential. Treat it as an appointment with yourself.
f. Use positive affirmations (talk to yourself): "This is what I am doing right now. It deserves all the attention I can give it. I know that there are other things that demand my attention, but this has got to be finished."

Thief 2—People

People often take a lot of your time without giving any value for your most precious resource. Here are some suggestions to minimize time stolen by people.

1. *Keep a time log.* Most CPAs usually do this. However, you may want to keep a separate log of the number of times you are interrupted by *people* during the day. This will tell you how much time is being stolen from

you. After you are convinced, you can drop the time log except as you need it for billing purposes.

2. *Use a calendar to schedule your day.* Compare your to-do list with your calendar. Block off times when you will work on the tasks on your list.

3. *Close your office door.* Forget the myths about open-door policy. You won't appear as unfriendly or aloof, just efficient. You work on intricate, complicated projects that are time sensitive. Each of your clients deserves your undivided attention. You can open your door when you are working on less complicated projects and interruptions won't disturb you. You can also have a regularly scheduled open door time for staff to come in with questions. Just tell your employees that clients are paying for your time, and they deserve all of it. A 30-second interruption during the preparation of a complicated tax return can cause a 20-minute delay in recapturing your train of thought. In addition to delay, it can cause errors and omissions.

4. *Conclude all visits as soon as possible.*
   - Stand up.
   - Stare at your work.
   - Use phrases such as, "Thanks for bringing that to my attention," or "glad I could help you, now what else can I do for you?"

5. *Manage client interruptions.* Clients, of course, deserve your service and attention. This pertains to *all* clients, not just those who drop by to see you without an appointment. In dealing with these types of interruptions, you must:
   - Use your staff effectively. They must have a list of VIP clients who will not interrupt unless it is important. They must also have a list of nuisance clients whom you want to avoid because you know they steal a lot of your time.
   - Use your invisible client. The invisible client is the one whose project you are working on but who isn't present. You are charging her for your time, so she deserves your complete attention. It is perfectly OK to have your staff say, "Jim is with a client right now. I am sure he would want to see you, though. If it is urgent, I can interrupt him. If not, may I set an appointment for you as soon as possible? Or can someone else help you?" Those questions will teach your nuisance clients to appreciate your time and will satisfy your good clients. If the client says it is urgent, go out of your office, close the door (leaving the invisible client inside), and converse with your VIP client in any available space other than your own office. This will guarantee to cut the visit short.

     Is this being deceptive to your clients? I think not. How about the invisible client? She brings in her tax return faithfully every year, lets you handle all of her investments, and seldom drops by except to pay her bill. Should her work be delayed or her bill increase because you were interrupted?

Thief 3—The Telephone

The telephone is essential to your business, just as people are. Here is how to make the telephone a tool rather than a thief.

1. *Screen your calls.* There are many top-level executives who pick up their own phones. Many believe that this adds a personal touch. I like to call someone who does this. However, people who can afford this luxury are usually not doers, they are strictly managers. Nor do they work directly on highly creative, complex tasks. They *manage* the people who work on these tasks. That allows them freedoms you and I may not enjoy. We have to be managers *and* doers. Therefore, I believe in screening calls. There are right ways and wrong ways to do this, however.

Here are some suggestions for the person to whom you have assigned the task of screening calls (in these examples, a receptionist).

Caller: "Is Jack there?"

(Wrong) "May I say who is calling?"

(Right) "Yes, he is here; he is with a client (or on the other line) right now." Always answer the question *before* you screen the call. Otherwise, it appears that whether or not Jack is in is determined by the degree of the caller's importance. After answering the question, then say, "I'm sure he will want to speak to you; I don't know how long he will be tied up. Shall I interrupt him or may I take a message and have him get back to you? How long are you going to be at this number?"

Caller: "No, don't interrupt him, just have him give me a call. How long do you think he will be tied up?"

(Right) The receptionist should know from Jack's calendar or instructions how long he will be tied up. "His calendar says that he has appointments back to back until noon. Will that be soon enough for a call back?"

Caller: "Yes, I need to speak to him for just a minute. Please interrupt him."

This is OK. Your caller knows that Jack is either on the phone or with another client. She will respect his time and keep the call short. Jack has been interrupted, but the client knows she is important and the interruption is minimal. This also saves a lot of "telephone tag."

Caller: "Please ask Jack to call me as soon as he can."

(Wrong) "May I tell him what this is concerning?" If the caller wanted to tell her business to the receptionist, she would have asked for the receptionist, not Jack. I know that this may screen out a few nuisance calls, but is it worth it when you alienate good clients? Ask yourself, "do I like to be screened like this?"

(Right) "Is there a file or other information I can pull for Jack so that he can be better prepared for your call?" This is about as far as one can go to get information about the call. Often, this single question will take care of the call. It will alert the receptionist to the nature of the call and may allow her to handle the call herself or give it to a staff member. Did you ever have a client leave an urgent message, only to find out later that all he wanted was to make an appointment to bring in his tax return—a task you will have to delegate to the person he talked to in the first place? Asking this question solves many such problems.

2. *Use telephone message pads.* Fill them out completely. Always have your receptionist get a return number and put it on the message form. If the client says "He has it," she should look it up and put it on the message anyway. You may indeed have the number, but it may require looking through files or Rolodexes for a minute or so. Every minute counts.

3. *Avoid telephone tag.* Your receptionist should be alerted when you are continually missing another party. It's up to you to stop the tag by taking the call and getting it over with.

4. *Keep your calls short and productive.* Try talking standing up. Use ending phrases, such as, "Thanks for the call, anything else I can help you with?" or "I know you are busy, so I won't keep you."

5. *Put a smile on your face;* it shows in your voice.

6. *Have the receptionist pull the file* and as much information as possible before returning the call. Especially during tax season, you should know the status of a return in-house, amount of refund, and so on before you make the call. This saves a lot of time and possibly a return call.

7. *Have a list of items you wish to cover* before you make a call. Check them off as you go. Everyone will appreciate your brevity and efficiency.

8. *Provide your receptionist with a VIP list* of people whose calls get priority.

9. *Have regular times each day* when you will take all calls, so that screening is not needed 100 percent of the time. Your clients will learn the best time to reach you. In addition, establish times when you will take only urgent calls.

10. *Designate a certain place* where phone messages will be placed. This should not be your in-box. It should not be on your desk. If your receptionist is constantly interrupting you to give you messages, you may as well be taking calls. I keep one spindle beside my in-box outside my office for incoming calls. A second spindle is on my desk for calls I have returned but which have not been yet resolved.

Thief 4—Your In-Box

I have problems with in-boxes. I can't resist getting into them and scattering their contents on my desk and in various other locations in my office. I am constantly emptying them before I am prepared to do anything with the contents. Here are some of the ways I improve on these time-wasting habits.

1. Locate your in-box outside your office and out of your sight if possible. Otherwise, you will constantly be glancing up when someone puts

something in it. In my prior office arrangement, the box was just outside my door. I could see it when my door was open. I could even hear someone put something in it when my door was closed. I couldn't resist the temptation to see what it was. The result? Interruptions, lack of focus, and wasted time. I moved it to an adjoining room and go to it only when I am prepared to work on its contents.

2. Have an urgent in-box on top of your regular in-box. This allows your staff to tell you what must be acted upon ASAP.

3. Keep a mail-out tray, a filing tray, and a work-out tray. This keeps your staff from confusing the categories.

4. Dump it, Delegate it, Do it, or Delay it. When you do schedule time for emptying your file tray, follow the four Ds:

Dump it. If it's junk mail, don't read it, no matter what tantalizing phrases are on the outside of the envelope. If you can't bring yourself to throw it away, then keep a basket beside your desk for those things you may want to look at later even if you're not sure they have any value. Those items you definitely want to keep for future reference but which require no action now, put in your "filling" tray.

Delegate it. If it is something that staff can handle, write a short note of instruction and put it in your work-out tray—*now*! I no longer have to write many of those notes. Staff knows what goes where.

Do it. If it is something that you can do in a few minutes, treat it like a saddle burr and do it *now*. Try to handle things of this type only once.

Delay it. *Delay* is not a good word, but is used to refer to items that come to your in-box that can't be done now, can't be delegated, and can't be thrown away. *Delay* doesn't mean to put it on a pile on your desk or in the corner of your office. Here are some examples of action steps for this type of item.

- Reading material—Add to your reading file, which should be kept in your briefcase.
- Tasks—Add the task to your task list and to your calendar if applicable.
- Seminars to attend and similar notices—I usually add these to my computer calendar and put the "physical" invitation, materials, and so forth on my desk calendar for the particular date in question (or a few days before the deadline for registering).
- Tax returns to review and similar items—Put these items inside a red, green, or yellow plastic folder indicating the level of priority. Place the folders on a side table or bookshelf. I like to use vertical file stands so that the projects will be in plain sight. A red folder alerts me to look at its contents and act on them soon.

What about the mounds of reading material that come across your desk?

How can you possibly absorb them? Unfortunately, you cannot. You need to focus on a few product groups and only glance at the others. You must at least speed read a large portion of the material, however. Don't spend an hour reading *The Wall Street Journal* or the daily paper every morning. Above all, don't use these as excuses for not getting to work. They too can be great thieves of time.

I try to catch the news on morning TV while I do preliminary exercises or on my radio on the way to work. There isn't enough time to read the daily papers from cover to cover. You are better off devoting an hour a day to reading time early in the morning or late at night. Concentrate on periodicals or books on the profession. This book has listed many periodicals and books to read.

Thief 5—Lost Files

Looking for files is the purest form of wasting time. Here are some ways to keep this problem under control.

1. *Keep your filing current.* If you put off filing because of the work load (for instance, during tax season), you will continually have trouble. Filing 50 files can take much less time than searching for one.

2. *Color code your files.* If you have separate colors for various categories of files, you are much less likely to misfile. Anyone will notice that a green folder should not be filed in a drawer filled with red ones.

3. *Maintain a file directory.* The directory should show the categories of files with appropriate colors and locations.

4. *Label the outside of your file drawers* and color code the labels to match the contents. This is an obvious step, but often overlooked.

5. *Don't allow yourself or others to keep files* in their offices for prolonged periods of time.

6. When a file is removed, *have a cardboard replacement ready to show its proper location.* The cardboard sheet should have a column for the file name and a column for the name of the person who is checking it out and the date.

7. *Use a temporary system for items that have not yet been reviewed.* Use open vertical file holders to hold red (high priority), green (next priority), and yellow (low priority) see-through plastic folders.

Thief 6—TV

Television is chief among pure wasters of time. Most of what we watch on television is drivel. It cannot even be classified as escapism, which we all need now and them. Most weekly programs are 30 percent commercials.

By eliminating the habit of flopping on the couch after the evening meal and watching three hours of cotton candy for the mind, I gained my largest block of time for improvement. The VCR was my salvation. It can allow you, too, to cut back substantially on TV watching.

Thief 7—Meetings Without Agendas

Need I say more?

Thief 8—Reinventing the Wheel

When you do something that is a little different, complex, or better, *document the process*. The next time it comes up, you won't have to go through the same efforts. This is especially important in regard to particular knowledge or skills gained by your staff. If one staff member leaves, be sure that there is a "trail" for the successor.

THE TOOLS OF TIME MANAGEMENT

So far, this chapter has covered the essentials of managing time:

1. The importance of setting goals.
2. Making and keeping lists and the various types of lists to keep.
3. Managing other people's time as well as your own.
4. The thieves of time and how to keep them away from your precious resource.

Here are some of the tools of time management that may have been previously referred to, with additional tips on their uses.

Tool 1—Calendars

You should have at least two calendars. One is for your appointments, and the other is to hold the physical items—invitations to seminars and so forth. Many people use time management calendars such as Day-Timers. Although both of my calendars lent themselves to the practice of time management, I did not use them for that purpose. For my CPA practice, I had a third appointment calendar that was kept with the receptionist to make my appointments. She would make the appointment on her calendar, then give me an appointment note to post to mine. She would compare and update both calendars daily.

I now use a computer calendar and a desk calendar. The computer calendar is used for all appointments and reminders, and the desk calendar holds my physical reminders for various events.

Tool 2—Lists

Refer to the eight basic lists covered in Chapter 19.

Tool 3—Color-Coded Files

Covered in a previous section of this chapter.

Tool 4—The In-Box

The in-box is a great tool as well as a thief of time. See "Thief 4" earlier in this chapter.

Tool 5—The Mini-Recorder

I use a small tape recorder for several purposes:

1. To dictate messages to my assistant or to myself.
2. To dictate letters and memos to be transcribed.
3. To listen to a tape of my goals on the way to work.
4. To use as a second memory when I travel. It is easier to enter something on a recorder than to try to decipher a hastily handwritten note on the back of a business card. Because I can talk a lot faster than I can write, this allows me to enter a lot more information.
5. To dictate specific notes about tax returns that were prepared. The recorder helps me to remember how I prepared a return and what I need to know for next year. These tapes are later transcribed and added to the top of the clients' files.

Tool 6—Capture the Moment During Tax Season

No one will disagree that tax season is a very busy time for tax professionals. We used to operate like a "well-oiled machine" during February, March, and April. We were at least three times as productive as we were during the rest of the year. I didn't want to work that hard all year, but I did want to be able to sustain some of the efficiency and enthusiasm that came with tax season. I usually came up with my best ideas and plans during tax season. Since there was no time to implement them, however, they very often faded from my mind. When I needed to recall them in the off-season, I could remember only a few. Here are some of the tools I used to capture those ideas without taking excessive time. I emphasize, however, that the time-saving techniques presented in this book should allow you the ability to act on many of the ideas *during tax season*.

The Big Sheet/Idea Folder. I keep a big stack of 8-1/2 by 11 paper within reach of where I work. When an idea comes to me that I can't implement right away, I write that idea down in a few key words or phrases and place the sheet in a tax season follow-up folder. On about April 20, I start reviewing this file and prioritize. I then add to my task list.

Why big sheets? Because the business cards, paper napkins, and small scraps of paper I used to use tend to get lost. In addition, notes are hard to read when they are written on small sheets.

The Investment Prospect Report. When I first started selling financial products, I saw many opportunities for financial planning as I prepared tax returns and visited with clients. I tried to act on these ideas during tax season. When that was not possible, I completed an Investment Prospect Report. The IPR was routed and placed in the client's investment file. Check-off points on the IPR provided for the task to be added to the central task system. When the task came due, I pulled the file and reviewed my notes on the IPR to refresh my memory of my ideas and what was discussed with the client. These keep good leads from being missed and make you look a lot smarter to the client.

Tool 7—Taped Audio Cassettes

Listening to audiocassettes is a great way to learn while you are driving. This makes maximum use of time that is otherwise unproductive.

Tool 8—Condensed Book Services

There are services that review books in your field. They write short reviews and condensed versions of the key points in the books.

Tool 9—Binder for Business Cards

I have found that a binder with alphabet tabs for holding business cards is a valuable resource that saves time in searching for addresses and other information.

Tool 10—Marketing and Technical Information Binders

We set up binders in our office for various categories of technical aspects of financial planning, as well as marketing aspects. As we come across articles or information of interest or value on a subject, we copy it for these centralized binders.

Other Helpful Hints to Conserve Time

1. Don't write your own checks. Sign them—but don't write them. Bills with prepared checks should be presented to you ready for your signature.
2. Take reading material with you at all times. Read on airplanes, in waiting rooms, and so forth.
3. Do your toughest work during the best part of your day.
4. Know when to quit. If you are getting fuzzy or overtired, stop and

get some rest. Sleeping can not only leave you refreshed, but can provide ideas and new perspective.

5. Know when to work more. If you are consistently overwhelmed even though you are using good time management, you may need to start a little earlier or stay a little later to work uninterrupted. Time spent in uninterrupted work is worth four to five times the time spent during regular working hours.

6. Read only the articles that interest you in periodicals. Copy them or cut them out, and file them in the marketing and publications binders if you think you will want to refer to them again.

By now you know why you must manage time. You know the basic steps to getting control of this valuable resource: deciding to do it, setting goals, and making lists. You know how to make lists and how to use them, as well as how to manage the time of people on your staff. I have given tips on delegating and how to attack the "thieves of time." I have presented several tools and hints on how to apply them. How much time are you going to save, and what are you going to do with it?

Savings

Setting goals, making and keeping lists	15 hours per week
Stopping the thieves of time	15–20 hours per week
Other hints and tools	5 hours per week

You can now save 40 hours per week! Assuming that you were already using half of these ideas, then you can save 20 hours. What are you going to do with this time? Here are my suggestions:

1. If you are doing financial planning as a sideline to your core business, then use this time to move it up to at least an equal footing with your other business. Done correctly, it will make you more total money for less effort than your current practice does.

2. Read books and periodicals on financial planning. If you read only one hour a day for one year, you will be good in this profession. Do it for two years, and you will be above your peer group. Three years, and you will be an expert; four years, and you will be a nationally known authority. Why not start today? Read one book a month and you will rank in the top 1 percent of your profession.

3. Set aside blocks of time on your calendar for thinking, creating, and planning. Keep a folder of notes for these times to spark the creative process. Find a quiet, secluded spot where you can be alone. Sit down, go through relaxation techniques, and clear your mind. Try to not think about anything for half an hour. That's very difficult. Don't worry about the ideas. They will come. You will get better at this every time you do it.

4. Attend more seminars and workshops in the financial planning profession.
5. Join professional associations and attend meetings and conventions.
6. Take more leisure time. Pleasure and productivity are not mutually exclusive when it comes to the use of our time. The 24 hours each of us gets each day comes around only once. Squeeze every drop of pleasure, knowledge, and productivity you can get from them.

Can we do it all—read one hour on professional subjects a day, review goals, spend a half hour thinking, make lists, exercise; enjoy leisure, family time, religion, community service, and work? When we consider all these things, there is certainly a tendency to freeze and do nothing. Yet it may sound more difficult than it is. Practicing time management just becomes a good habit after a short period of time. Look at the alternatives and the benefits—it's worth it.

21

The Mind-Body Relationship

FINDING ENERGY WHEN THERE IS NONE

I know that I have to be cautious when talking about the mind-body relationship in a book written for financial professionals. We're not going to talk about faith healing, at least not in the context in which we ordinarily think of it in our Western culture. We are going to discuss how the physical condition of your body affects your overall health and vice versa. I don't know which comes first, I just know there is a link.

"How do you know?" you ask. Most CPAs and other tax professionals interview thousands of people during the course of a career. I personally conducted more than 6,000 interviews during the period when I was a practicing CPA. My clients and I used to compare my services to those of a personal physician. The tax interview can be extremely personal. We often gather data about medical and other types of expenses that reveal intimate details of clients' lives. We are trusted to keep these details confidential. Many times we serve as counselors, even though we may be unwilling and unqualified. During the course of these interviews, I began noticing a definite link between the mind and body. Clients who thought of themselves as healthy invariably were. Clients who "predicted" health problems invariably turned out to be accurate as well.

There were many examples, but I will tell of one. I happened to have two clients near the same age with approximately the same income. They both had serious back problems. Both scheduled identical surgery at about the same time. One told me that he expected to recover just fine and generally had a positive worldview. The other, a constant "victim" with a negative worldview, told me that the "quacks" would probably cripple him. I didn't see either client for another year. Sure enough, when the fellow with the positive view came in to have his return prepared the following year, he was in great spirits and said he never felt better. I was astonished to see the other client two weeks later. He came to the office stooped at a 90-degree angle, carrying a cane. He could hardly speak. He told me he had filed a suit against the physician. I know that an isolated incident proves nothing. However, this type of experience had been observed many times before.

The evidence was enough for me to start forming opinions about the direct link between mental health and physical health. Please don't conclude that I believe that all illness is psychological. I do firmly believe, however, that good mental health is essential to physical health. I also believe that the mind exerts a great deal of control over our physical health.

The Chinese have believed for 2000 years that the mind and emotions maximize health. The ancient art of t'ai chi is entering mainstream America today. Sigmund Freud said that "illness begins in the mind." Highly acclaimed journalist Bill Moyers authored the book *Healing and the Mind* and hosted a five-part series on the subject on public television.

What does all this have to do with CPAs adding financial planning to their practices? Everything! Being in the best possible shape physically is an essential ingredient to reaching what I call the "power zone." Professional athletes call it "the flow." It's what Roger Staubach was experiencing during those incredible come-from-behind victories for the Dallas Cowboys. The power zone is defined as the area of success in any endeavor that most people never reach. I am not talking about "runner's high" or iron-man marathons. I am talking about the state of consciousness reached when you know that you can achieve success at much higher levels than you ever dreamed possible. The zone is beyond the reach of people who elect to omit *any* of the essential ingredients of goal setting, time management, and good physical condition. The zone requires intense visualization prior to the event and intense focus when the event actually takes place.

Let me add some qualifications. If you are a marathon runner, skip to the next chapter. You are already in good shape. You already know that your body is a "temple." These tips are for the CPA who has been treating his body as something less than a temple and gives his used car more routine maintenance.

FOLLOWING BASIC RULES

As with many other secrets to success, the rules are fairly simple.

1. Set goals.
2. Visualize how you will look and feel when you reach your goals.
3. Eat sensibly.
4. Exercise regularly.
5. Develop good habits and change bad habits.

Of course, we learned rules 3 and 4 in grade school. Then why don't we follow these rather sensible precepts. The reason is that they go against the basic human inclination toward instant gratification and away from pain.

> The inability to delay instant gratification is a predictor of failure. People do what is "fun and easy" rather than what is hard and necessary.

Good health habits can be made a little more fun and easier by looking into the preceding five steps in more detail.

Set Goals

You should already be familiar with this important strategy. I suggest that you separate your physical goals into short-term and long-term. This is especially important if you are really pushing the outer limits of the weight chart for someone six inches taller than you or have trouble walking to your car. If you set a goal to be in excellent physical shape within a year, you'll probably become discouraged in the second week. Take it a week or two at a time. Set a goal to exercise three times the first week and cut out all desserts. The next week, try exercising four times a week and limiting coffee to two cups per day, still leaving out desserts.

Give yourself rewards for accomplishment—perhaps a no-fat yogurt cone.

Keep adding to your short-term goals until you reach your long-term goals. If you fall behind or slip up a time or two, forgive yourself and go right back into working toward your goals.

Visualize

Picture how you will look and feel after you have reached your goals. Start thinking of yourself as you would like to be. Don't continually remind yourself of what you have allowed yourself to become. Remember, this is the beginning of the new you.

Think positively. If a "bug" is going around, keep telling yourself that your immune system is too strong to allow this weak germ inside your body.

Eat Sensibly

After reading several books on proper diet, I became thoroughly confused with good and bad cholesterol, calories, and fat grams. As much as I love good food, I knew I would never count all the things you need in order to stay on a balanced diet. I needed one thing to watch out for. When a friend referred me to a book called the *The T-Factor Diet*, I decided that the culprit was fat grams. Besides, it made sense to my practical mind—fat grams make you fat. I ordered a "Fat Guide" from the Center for Science in the Public Interest and began to use the small slide rule they gave me to learn about fat grams. I now mentally check the fat grams on just about everything before I indulge. Unless your physician has instructed you otherwise, the following tips can help in any approach to sensible eating:

1. Watch fat grams.
2. Eat lots of fruit and vegetables.
3. Drink lots of water.
4. Eat more often but less. Don't skip meals.
5. Don't smoke.
6. Drink in moderation if at all.

Eating sensibly requires cultivating good habits. It isn't easy to change old ways, but the rewards are great.

Exercise Regularly

My favorite words are *commitment* and *persistence*. Make a commitment to do something and stick to it. Nike commercials have expressed it very well: "Just do it!"

The different forms of exercise that are best for you and how they should be used can be determined between you and your doctor.

For most people, the type of exercise doesn't matter, as long as it increases heart rate and keeps it to that level for at least 20 minutes, three times a week. That's routine maintenance. If you need to lose weight or want to get in top condition, it may take about 30 minutes four times a week. If you want to eat more, then you may have to add a long walk over the weekend.

I have invested thousands of dollars over the past several years in looking for the perfect exercise machine: one that will make me lose weight, keep me from becoming bored, and doesn't involve pain. There is no such machine. I have found best results with exercises that don't involve machines. Most are very simple—push-ups and sit-ups, walking and jogging. When my office was only three minutes from a racquetball court, I found the perfect exercise for me. It fueled my competitive spirit, kept my reflexes sharp, and relieved my tensions. Now that a racquetball game takes at least two hours out of my day, I can no longer participate. Yet that has not kept me from my commitment to exercise. Until I can get back on the court, I have reverted to my other machines—my arms and legs.

The type of exercise you choose depends on a number of factors, among which are the time available and personal preference.

When should you exercise? Strange as it may seem, I once found noontime to be the best for me. It broke the day in half and seemed to work better for weight control. Since that option is not available now, I exercise early in the morning; late afternoon is the last choice.

Choose the best time available to you and, as much as possible, use the same time each day you schedule for exercise.

Develop Good Habits and Change Bad Habits

Developing good habits is a goal in almost any aspect of life: financial, spiritual, and physical. We are all encumbered by bad habits. Good habits can be formed to take their place if we practice. Remember—commit and persist.

Self-discipline came easily to me in work and study. Good habits in exercise were a little more difficult. But I made a commitment, changed my attitude, and just did it. When a good habit gets monotonous or boring for you, try some positive thinking. For instance, recite your physical goals over and over as you exercise. Recite your other goals, also. *Now that's good time management.*

22

Using Your "Other Mind"

THE POWER OF THE SUBCONSCIOUS

I can already hear the question—Why is a CPA writing about the power of the subconscious? I know that I am in dangerous territory.

That doesn't bother me. What bothers me is that I am writing about a subject that I am not qualified to write about. In this chapter I use a number of personal stories and quotations from people much more qualified to write on the subject than I. A chapter on the subconscious was necessary for this book, because I found that new discoveries I had made regarding the subconscious were the key to truly getting me out of my comfort zone and into the power zone. Remember, the power zone is more than getting out of your comfort zone. It is that state of mind in which you feel capable of doing things you never thought possible.

What is the subconscious mind and what does it do? I have heard of the subconscious mind most of my life. I thought of it as that portion of the brain just below the surface that takes care of those "automatic" things, such as breathing, heartbeat, digestion, and so on. I also thought that it sent messages to the conscious mind whenever I got "too big for my britches." For example, I made excellent grades all the way from first grade through the ninth. However, I kept hearing a little voice that said, "It's because you secretly worked harder than everyone else and because you are going to a tiny school that is easier than the big ones." I believed that little voice. I worked hard because of a strange combination of a sense of inferiority and high competitiveness. We were very poor and I was smaller than average. (And the school *was* tiny.)

When I was a freshman in high school, we moved and I went from a class of 11 students to a class of 185. My parents were warned not to expect the same good grades that I had achieved in the small school. I finished my freshman year in the top 10 percent with straight As. The little voice said, "It's because you worked harder. A lot of the kids who didn't do as well are smarter."

I went to two more high schools and all the way through college with excellent grades. The voice never quit. I was fortunate enough to graduate when the economy was at a peak. Because of this and my good grades, I had more than 30 job offers after college. I took the one that had two qualifications—it looked relatively easy and it paid a good starting salary. My college professor said, "You'll be bored with this job." The little voice said, "Better take something easy, or they will find out that you are not as smart as your grades say you are." That little voice that I erroneously identified as my subconscious kept sending me those negative messages all the way through several other jobs and into the period when I opened my own practice. Then I began to find out that the little voice was coming from my *conscious* mind, sending messages to my subconscious. This was when I learned that the subconscious does do all those automatic things, but it also receives and acts upon messages that the conscious mind sends it. That changed my whole way of thinking. It was my conscious mind that was keeping me from getting out of my comfort zone, not my subconscious. Although I was correct in thinking that the subconscious was the more powerful, I was incorrect in thinking that I had no control over it and that it always sends the correct signals.

> The greatest discovery of the nineteenth century was not in the realm of physical science. It was the power of the subconscious touched by faith.
> —William James, father of American psychology

> The mind is the limit. As long as the mind can envision the fact that you can do something, you can do it—as long as you really believe 100 percent.
> —Arnold Schwarzenegger

> What the mind can conceive and believe, the mind of man can achieve.
> —Napoleon Hill

> What this power is I cannot say, all I know is that it exists and it becomes available only when a man is in that state of mind in which he knows exactly what he wants and is fully determined not to quit until he finds it.
> —Alexander Graham Bell

Right brained or left brained? I know that my audience is primarily made up of CPAs and other "left-brained people." The left hemisphere of the brain is the rational, logical side. It controls the functions of calculation, logic, verbal articulation, structured observation, analysis, and the like. The right side performs nonrational functions such as intuition, pattern recognition, nonverbal communication, abstraction, and so on. I assure you that I am a left-brained person: "If it ain't logical, if I can't see it; if you can't prove it, don't talk to me about it." If I can make use of the subconscious after 40 years of this type of thinking, anyone can.

Synthesist, realist, analyst, pragmatist, or idealist? Many of you have taken the tests to determine whether you are a synthesist, realist, analyst, pragmatist, or idealist. In learning to use the subconscious, I have changed from a high analyst and realist to a high idealist and pragmatist within eight years. If you have not taken the test, you may want to purchase *The Art of Thinking* by Allen Harrison and Robert Bramson.

Faith and the subconscious. In his book, *The Power of Your Subconscious Mind*, Joseph Murray describes "scientific" prayer as "the harmonious interaction of the conscious and subconscious levels of mind scientifically directed for a specific purpose. . . . The answer to prayer results when the individual's subconscious mind responds to the mental picture or thought in the mind. This law of belief is operating in all religions of the world and is the reason why they are psychologically true. . . . As a man *thinks*, *feels*, and *believes*, so is the condition of his *mind*, *body*, and *circumstances*."

Most of those who rarely, if ever, wonder about prayer or faith have at least some sense of a power greater than themselves. They may, as I did, use these principles to strengthen their search:

1. You must believe in a power greater than yourself and that you can use that power through both levels of your mind.

2. The subconscious obtains its great power through faith and reliance on this greater power.

3. The subconscious is powerful but cannot reason. It acts to bring about circumstances and events, as you instruct it through your conscious mind. Your conscious mind is the watchdog. It functions to protect your subconscious from false impressions. Therefore, it can work for or against you. It was that little voice speaking to me, because I taught it what to say.

4. Changing negative thought patterns and negative habits into positive ones will send the same type of messages to your subconscious.

5. You can train yourself to send the right signals to your subconscious.

6. Goals are the key elements in training your subconscious.

7. It is OK to train yourself to think of yourself as something you want to be, rather than what you may be at present.

8. The power works completely only when you think good thoughts of and provide service to others. This belief was important to my acceptance of the power, because the logic of my conscious mind kept saying, "If this is true, can't evil people use this power too?"

USING THE DUALITY OF YOUR MIND

The following paragraphs provide practical ideas for using the duality of your mind—the conscious and the subconscious.

1. Watch what you say! I am grateful to my parents for shaming me every time I said *can't*. My dad used to say, "There is no such word as *can't* if you believe you can." Don't say, "I can't afford it" or "I don't have time." Your subconscious mind takes you at your word and sees to it that what you say and believe comes true. Remember this—your subconscious mind can't take a joke.

2. You have the capacity to choose. Choose happiness, health, and wealth over sadness, illness, and poverty.

3. Practice. Really having a choice means practicing your faith in yourself and continually sending positive thoughts to your subconscious. Stop all negative thoughts in their tracks.

4. Believe. Believe that you can achieve the goals you have listed for yourself.

5. Visualize. A mental picture is worth a thousand words. Your subconscious mind will bring to reality any picture held in the mind backed by *faith*.

6. Relax. Don't try to focus the issue. You can't coerce your conscious mind to change thought patterns at once. You must get into a relaxed, even sleepy or drowsy, state in order to send the messages.

7. Use positive affirmations. They will work only if you repeat them using items 1 through 6.

8. Build a new body. Change your body by changing your thoughts and keeping them changed.

9. Forget the myths about wealth. Because we were poor, I grew up believing that most wealth was ill-gotten and the misquote "Money is the root of all evil." Such myths keep us from attaining wealth. There is no virtue in poverty. Claim your right to be rich. Money is only a symbol, but acquiring money is necessary to lead a balanced life and to have the freedom to do all the things you want to do when you want to do them.

10. Rely on your "invisible means of support." Most people will never take a job where they are paid strictly on commission or what they produce because they have no "invisible means of support." The only true job security lies within yourself.

11. Don't expect something for nothing. You must give mental as well as physical attention to your goals, your ideas, and your business. You must go about your work and the progressive achievement of your goals with the idea of wealth in your mind.

Although the power of the subconscious touched with faith was discovered in the nineteenth century, it became real to me only a few years ago. My belief in this power, the discovery that I could control it, that I could make choices, was critical to goal achievement and success, and to entry into the power zone.

23

Finding Time to Increase Profits in Your Practice (Adding Financial Planning and Products)

Earlier, this book discussed good time management practices. This chapter deals more specifically with how to add financial planning and products to what appears to be an already crowded schedule. The subject of time management is covered once again because it is the chief concern of CPAs who are considering the addition of another profit center to their practices.

Most of the CPAs I have trained or worked with are jealous entrepreneurs. They built their practices based on personal service to their clients and are understandably reluctant to do anything that might jeopardize that relationship. Unfortunately, more than 75 percent of the CPAs I have worked with are also notoriously poor managers of time. Only attorneys, who also sell time, are worse.

This book has explained in some detail why most CPA firms must add this service in order to remain competitive and *retain* their current clients. After accepting this fact, most CPAs have two further concerns:

1. Am I in danger of damaging client relationships?
2. How do I find time when I am overworked now?

The rest of this chapter addresses these issues.

DELEGATING

The value of delegating has been discussed earlier in a more general context. CPAs are notoriously poor delegators for many reasons, a few of which are examined in the following paragraphs.

1. "Clients want *me* to do it!" You're absolutely right. You also would like the top lawyer in the firm to work on finding your lost birth certificate. You would like the top surgeon in the hospital to work on your hangnail. You want the best mechanic in the dealership to change your spark plugs. However, if that happens, I will show you inefficient legal and health practices and a poorly run auto dealership. Your clients will understand when you do not perform every detail of a project for them. In fact, I found that my clients respected my time more after I started delegating some client contact to staff.

2. "The work I do is too complex to trust to subordinates." Admit it—about 50 percent of what you are doing could be done by someone with less than two years of experience in the business. I think you know that many of the types of returns you do are currently being prepared through a "chain" tax preparation service by clerks with only six weeks' training. Moreover, software is now good enough to rely on in most cases. Will others do the job as well or as fast as you? Probably not, at least in the beginning. But if you have procedures in place for proof and control and

have conveyed to staff your commitment to quality, then they will do it to the customers' satisfaction.

3. "I don't have any subordinates." Calculate the maximum amount you can earn if you are able to bill 60 percent of your total time. If that is enough for you, you are doomed to stay in your comfort zone. If you want to earn more, then hire someone.

4. "It takes too long to train staff." It does take a long time, and sometimes it can be frustrating. However, if you want to grow and want to know that your practice could go on at least for a period of time if you were ill, then you must have trained staff. Besides, almost all of us will someday tire of dealing with minutiae.

5. "My clients will be hurt when I tell them. I can't face my clients and tell them that someone else will be dealing with them. It's like saying I have outgrown them. Their feelings will be hurt." This is a difficult situation. However, I described the problem to a few of my best clients, and they all understood. They suggested that I write a letter explaining the reasons for the change. I did this and even made a video of myself explaining our changes to play in the lobby. Use these reasons:

a. Computers have changed the way you do business. The *very expensive* software you have purchased is so good that calculation errors are almost nonexistent. That allows you to use staff for some of the things you used to do.

b. The organizer provided has a list of almost foolproof questions that your highly trained staff can go through to be sure that nothing is left to chance.

c. Your staff is highly trained and eager to accept more responsibility and client contact. If you don't give it to them, they will seek it elsewhere. Besides, they are ready.

d. You have to do everything possible to slow the increase in fees. (Notice I didn't mention no increase, nor decrease.) Since your clients are aware that your time is the most expensive in the office, they will get the picture.

e. Tax laws have changed, making it necessary to change your method of operation. (Don't tell them that their tax returns have become so simple that anyone could do them.)

f. Ask the client, "Would you prefer the highest-paid person in the place to look at your return to be sure it is correct *after* it has been input and go over it in detail with you, or would you rather that person spend billable time going through supporting data *before* it is prepared?"

g. If you can delegate staff to the pre-interview and input on the computer, you can devote more time to making sure the return was done correctly and go over it in detail with the client when it is finished.

h. At the request of your clients and in response to very evident needs in the marketplace, you have expanded your services to include a more thorough analysis of your clients' tax returns in order to give advice on what actions they should take to reduce their taxes and reach their financial goals in coming years. In the past, you have been a *reporter* of past events; now, you will not only advise clients about their current returns, you will also be able to assist them in taking steps toward their goals of reduced taxes and increased financial security in future years.

If a client insists on doing business the same old way, in spite of these reasons, then assure him he can. Most will cooperate. For those who don't, see the section "Rating Clients" later in this chapter.

6. "I can't find good employees." This is a tough one. Finding people who can survive in the world of small business is difficult, much less finding those who will prosper. In interviewing employees, I use the acronym EARRS to remember the primary traits I am looking for.

- E is for Enthusiasm. Prospective employees must have enthusiasm. It must be evident in their smile, walk, and talk.
- A is for Attitude. Applicants must answer questions with the right attitude. The attitude must be one of willingness to learn and to cooperate. They must understand the necessity to sacrifice in order to gain. They should have goals that they can articulate to you. They should know that a price may have to be paid in terms of hard work and some personal sacrifice in order to attain those goals. Are they willing to pay the price to get what they want? They should know that 40 hours per week is for sustenance, more than 40 is for success.
- R is for Resourcefulness. I find this quality lacking in many good candidates. It is the ability to reach out of their comfort zone and to gather together all the resources at their disposal to finish a project, even if it is unfamiliar to them. I like associates who are not afraid to ask dumb questions to anyone who might have information available needed to get the project finished. They will look in files, search through computer information, make phone calls, and so forth to learn everything there is to know about the project and how to complete it. The next time it is assigned, they will know how to do it better than you do. Employees who rely on you for specific instructions as to where to find all the information they need, whom to call, and what to say, will not remember as well the next time the project comes up. Clear instructions are important, but small businesses often cannot function the way large businesses can. Entrepreneurs often are not prone to giving detailed instructions; they expect employees to be resourceful.
- R is for Responsibility. Most employees are taught in high school, college, and in seminars to avoid accepting responsibility for what

happens to them. They are taught to place blame on other people and events. Not enough training, unclear instructions, long hours, and such are given as the reasons for poor performance. Find employees who take responsibility for everything that happens to them. They can't control all events, but they can control their reactions to them. Most can find the source of their problems by looking in the mirror. (The same is true for all of us.)

- S is for Skills. Even if the EARR qualities are present, you may not be able to hire an applicant if he or she needs specialized training to handle the job that is open. If computer skills are lacking, but are required, then keep interviewing until you get them.

RATING CLIENTS

I have been to many practice management seminars where I was told to rate my clients and heard bold talk about "firing clients." I seldom saw a need to actually fire a client. Perhaps it would be more accurate to say that I could seldom bring myself to fire a client. However, rating clients does become more important if you are going to add both new products and services. You might consider categorizing clients as follows:

1. *Clients who are slow to pay.* Follow a simple rule: Don't get in any deeper. Before you do any more work, require a reduction of the prior balance and payment in advance for the work you are about to perform. Estimate the fee high. Delegate all work done for these clients to staff. You can't afford to work for them.
2. *Clients who don't pay at all.* They usually won't be back. If they come back, require payment in advance and a full payment of old balances. Delegate future work.
3. *Clients who complain about fees regularly.* A perfect reason to delegate their work. The only alternatives are to raise their fees until they leave or fire them.
4. *Clients who don't follow rules,* observe appointments, or follow your advice or who procrastinate. Raise their fees. Delegate their work.

A, B, C Clients. After you have identified all of the preceding client types and acted accordingly, go through your entire client list and rate your clients as A, B, C in overall importance to your firm. You need to do whatever it takes to please your A clients as long as you can ethically do it and it is profitable. B clients should be delegated to your highest-level staff. You should seldom, if ever, see C clients other than to say hello.

1, 2, 3 Clients. Go through your clients and rate them again as to their viability as financial planning prospects. *Caution*—I have been amazed when CPAs do this and identify only about 5 percent of their clients as financial planning prospects. I found 85 percent to be prospects: 30 percent were 1s, 40 percent were 2s, and 15 percent were 3s. Seventy-five percent actually turned into financial planning clients.

Since you have a close relationship with your clients, you should be able to go through the entire rating process in only about 30 minutes for each 100 clients.

Of course, you can offer an excuse: "My clients just don't have any money." If that's true, which it isn't, then you have been doing a poor job of advising them. Is this a temporary condition or a permanent one? If they don't want it to be a permanent one, then they need your help.

Or you may complain: "I asked my clients whether they needed financial planning from me and they said no." Your question was probably, "You wouldn't want to buy any mutual funds from me, would you?" Of course the client said no. Approach your inquiry into financial planning matters with the same professionalism that you do in gathering tax data.

After you have finished rating your clients, complete a cover sheet for your tax file similar to the one provided earlier in this book. Alert your staff that you want to:

1. Do post-tax interviews with all the As and 1s. You may have to do pre-interviews with the As as well.
2. From the B list, delegate tax return preparation, including the pre-interview for at least 80 percent. Try to post-interview at least 80 percent (this may not be the same 80 percent). You should interview all the 1s, 80 percent of the 2s, and 35 percent of the 3s.
3. Neither interview nor prepare any returns for the C list. Post-interview 100 percent of the 1s, at least 50 percent of the 2s, and 20 percent of the 3s.

I caution you again to be careful when discounting someone as not being a financial planning prospect. Almost everyone is, should be, someday will be, or has a friend or relative who can be referred to you. How many people do you know who:

1. Couldn't reduce taxes by making some move or another with investments?
2. Don't need to retire earlier or wealthier than they would without your help?
3. Couldn't use assistance in setting up an education fund for a child or grandchild?
4. Don't have an estate tax problem?
5. Have the wrong kind or amount of insurance?
6. Have all their investments in too few or too many places?

7. Don't have or need an emergency fund?
8. Own a business but don't need help in setting up a retirement plan, transferring to heirs, or selling?
9. Have their wills, powers of attorney, and estate plans completely in order?

If some of your clients do not require these kinds of assistance, then they have a lot of money that you may be able to assist them with investing one day. It's worth it to let them know you are in the business if they ever need you. Compliment them on a job well done, and ask for referrals of people who are not as fortunate or astute as they.

Remember: Every one of your clients is a prospect for business or for a referral. Let them all know that you are in the business.

DECIDING WHAT YOU WANT TO BE AND DO

"You can't be all things to all people." That worn-out saying has been used as an excuse too many times for not leaving the comfort zone. I'm not suggesting that you be *all* things to all people. I am suggesting that you offer more than tax preparation and, possibly, write-up services to your clients. By itself, tax preparation is an inadequate service. In order for it to be more than just a negative service that the client compares to going to the dentist, it must be at least combined with tax planning (a quasi-positive service). I submit that if you don't add assistance in reaching a client's goals to your service repertoire, you are doing a disservice.

The nay-sayers who think that CPAs can't do more than one thing are wrong. Hundreds of CPAs have been assisting clients in identifying and reaching their financial goals while running profitable practices for many years. Who is better qualified? How many other financial advisors have the depth of knowledge about taxes and other financial aspects of your clients' lives that you do? How many see them at least once a year? How many are more concerned about meeting their needs than selling them a product?

We may not be all things to all people, but we can surely do more than any other professional group to help our clients to reach financial security.

I said earlier that one of the keys to success is deciding what you love to do and then doing it. Money will follow. If you love helping your clients to achieve their fondest hopes, dreams, and aspirations, then you owe them and yourself an obligation to get the training you need to assist them.

How much money will follow? Good question. Since industrywide statistics are impossible to get at this time, I can only quote from my own experience and from others with whom I have been involved.

Of my original clients, 75 percent also became clients of the new products and services.

The average revenue during the last three years per client was approximately $500.

Converted to a direct hourly rate, the earnings were approximately 400 percent of my regular billing rate for CPA services.

The key question: Do I want to be a reporter of events that have already taken place in my clients' lives, or do I want to be an active participant and advisor as well?

USING ASSISTANTS IN YOUR PRACTICE

Involve your assistants and staff in all phases of your financial planning practice from the first day. If it is too late for you to follow that advice, start involving them tomorrow. Except for the most efficient in time management, staff involvement is critical to enjoyment of the profession as well as to success.

Greeting Clients and Answering Calls

Get your clients involved with your staff from the first day. Introduce them and teach both the clients and your staff about the kinds of problems staff can handle without bothering you.

Setting Appointments

I hate setting appointments; therefore, I am not very good at it. So why should I do it? The nice thing about having a CPA practice is that you are not "cold" calling. Your receptionist can set appointments with your clients. A call from your staff during tax season is like a call from the president.

Handling Introductory Interviews

An introductory interview is an interview that takes place when a new client walks in off the street or a client comes in with her data but doesn't need to see a tax preparer. It consists of checking to see whether she brought prior year returns, filled out her organizer, has W-2s and so on. If she is woefully short, this interview can save a lot of time for you or your senior staff. Otherwise, the preparer will tear into the tax return and find that half of the data is missing—a waste of expensive time. I would rather use the receptionist's time (of course, try to bill for it if you can).

Asking a Few Key Questions

When a client comes in with his tax return data, we usually have someone hand him a sheet containing questions about his financial goals. The staff member will also tell him about our full-service financial planning available at no cost to him. We don't ask for an appointment, we just present it as a service that will be provided. After all, who would turn down a half hour of free time with a CPA? If a client says he doesn't want the service, then you know not to waste your time. For the wise client who doesn't turn down the offer, you will have the key information about his goals to discuss when you do the post-interview. At worst, the client will not be able to give the staff the information, or does not bring it back. At least, he will have had the chance to look at it and think about it. He can't claim surprise when you ask him about his goals again.

Gathering Data

Gathering data to do a small or large financial plan can be very difficult for a CPA who is used to having his or her clients trained to present data in a certain way. It can also be difficult for the client. He is embarrassed when he doesn't know what his goals are, what his risk tolerance is, and where his assets are located. He might be less embarrassed meeting with a staff person than with you. Staff are often better at extracting this critical information than I am. I talk too much, start to analyze each piece of data before I get the full picture, and let the client tell me long stories about each asset he owns. Thus, my notes and forms are often incomplete. Better to let the assistant do it.

Preparing Applications

Have your assistant licensed or at least fingerprinted so that he or she can work on applications. After you have mastered the art of application completion, delegate it. Dealing with the redundant and often confusing nature of the applications when involved in the sales process can be distracting. Your assistant should have the applications ready when the client comes in. You can review them before or after the client signs, or both. You can move on to the next sale. Remember, I only do what only I can do. I'm the best at making the sale. I need to spend my time doing just that.

Taking the Money

Separate yourself from the money. Let an assistant take it. Don't get involved in the question of ''Whom should I make this check out to'' or in writing the check yourself. It is too easy to sign your client's only check by mistake, thus delaying and possibly killing the sale.

In addition, keep these points in mind:

1. When you move the client to a different area from where the sale is completed and go on to another client, the client considers the transaction ended. There is much less likelihood that she will feel remorse and back out before you have done the paperwork.

2. Your client can get all his anxieties off his chest by talking with your assistant. After the emotion of making his buying decision with you, he will have plenty of time to justify it logically with a well-trained assistant to assure him. This also prevents a lot of buyer's remorse calls after you get home at night.

3. Risks can be explained again to your client in a nonthreatening environment. Your assistant should be provided with a standard form to complete for each transaction to ensure that the client clearly understands the risks you explained to her during the sales process. If the investment is going to make the client uncomfortable, better to find it out now than later. Moreover, your client will appreciate your openness and frankness in discussing these issues to ensure that she is fully informed.

4. A relationship is established between your assistant and your client in this transaction. Guess who will get the call when the client's name is spelled wrong or a Social Security number is input incorrectly? You don't want or need calls of this type.

5. Your assistant will establish an all-important network of people in the office who can solve your clients' problems quickly in your absence.

Affording Opportunities for Growth

One of the primary reasons for turnover in small CPA firms is lack of opportunity for growth. Using an assistant for a number of duties will offer that opportunity.

Training

Assistants should be offered training by you and through outside sources as well. Take your assistants with you to conferences. Send them to seminars and workshops.

Epilogue

The last ten years of my life have been spent practicing financial planning and teaching others how to practice it. Three years ago, I sold my CPA practice in order to devote full time to financial planning. Three months ago, I sold those same clients again as financial planning clients.

I have had the privilege of sharing my successes and failures with others through training sessions and by writing. I have had contact with more than 10,000 tax professionals during those years. Tax practices are certainly run using different approaches and methods. However, a common thread seems to run through them all—they are primarily historians and reporters of past events. They use the same excuses for not getting more involved in their clients' lives even when they recognize that their clients need help. Those excuses are always the same. Lack of time, lack of product knowledge, conflict of interest, independence. From those professionals who have moved out of their comfort zone in order to offer meaningful changes in people's lives, we learn that the real reasons for failure to act are fear and ignorance. Fear of leaving the comfort zone and lack of training in what it takes to be successful in financial planning. Through this book and the expanded *Financial Planning: The CPA's Practice Guide*, (also published by John Wiley & Sons, Inc.) I have attempted to offer the tools necessary to make you successful. If I can assist in any other way, please call me at 800–959–5999.

Index